CLEAN EATING SLOW COOKER FOR TWO

Jamie Stewart

Copyright © 2017

All Rights Reserved

All rights reserved. No part of this book may be reproduced or transmitted in any form or by any means, electronic or mechanical, including photocopying, recording or by any information storage and retrieval system, without written permission from the publisher, except for the inclusion of brief quotations in a review.

Warning-Disclaimer

The purpose of this book is to educate and entertain. The author or publisher does not guarantee that anyone following the techniques, suggestions, tips, ideas, or strategies will become successful. The author and publisher shall have neither liability or responsibility to anyone with respect to any loss or damage caused, or alleged to be caused, directly or indirectly by the information contained in this book.

CONTENTS

INTRODUCTION 7

   Grandma Knows Best 8

   Using Your Slow Cooker 11

   Pantry Staples for Better
   Cooking 12

VEGETABLES & SIDE DISHES .. 14

   1. Mushroom and Kale
   Breakfast Quiche..........................15

   2. Sunrise Cremini
   Mushrooms 16

   3. Breakfast Hash Brown
   Casserole 17

   4. Sunday Morning Asparagus
   Casserole 18

   5. Barley with Mushrooms and
   Scallions 19

   6. Lentil, Kale and Sweet
   Potato Soup................................... 20

   7. Cauliflower and Quinoa
   Soup 21

   8. Harvest Butternut Squash
   Stew 22

   9. Aunt's Broccoli and Quinoa
   Soup 23

   10. The Best Pumpkin Bisque
   Ever.. 24

   11. Easy Curried Cauliflower
   Soup 25

   12. Potato and Carrot Potage 26

   13. Dilled Vegetable Soup 27

   14. Hot Mixed Vegetable Stew 28

   15. Light Saucy Eggplant............. 29

   16. Hot Stuffed Peppers with
   Cauliflower 30

   17. Pepper and Hominy Stew 31

   18. Rainbow Mushroom Soup 32

   19. Baked Potato Appetizer 33

   20. Bavarian Cabbage with
   Apples 34

CHICKEN 35

   21. Chicken Chili Beans 36

   22. Tandoori-inspired Pulled
   Chicken...37

   23. Tangy Mesquite Chicken 38

   24. Party Chicken Wings with
   Honey and Ketchup 39

   25. Cherry-Glazed Chicken
   Wings... 40

   26. Chicken with Jalapeño and
   Beans 41

   27. Moroccan-Style Tomato
   and Chicken Stew 42

   28. Chicken, Orzo and
   Kale Soup 43

   29. Chicken and Root Vegetable
   Soup 44

   30. Chicken Stew with
   Potatoes and Corn 45

   31. Habanero Chicken Chili 46

32. Old-Fashioned Roasted Chicken with Vegetables 47

33. Easiest Barbecue Chicken Ever 48

34. Tangy 'n' Sweet Chicken Wings................................. 49

35. Peppery Chicken Curry 50

36. Ginger Chicken Thighs 51

37. Sticky Chicken Drumsticks ... 52

38. Honey-Glazed Chicken Wings 53

39. Italian Sausage and Chicken in Tomato Sauce 54

40. Greek-Style Chicken Stew 55

TURKEY 56

41. Turkey and Mushroom Chowder 57

42. Hot Peppery Turkey Soup with Corn 58

43. Hominy and Turkey Chili 59

44. Zucchini Noodles with Turkey and Vegetables 60

45. Turkey Chili with Cheddar Cheese 61

46. Turkey, Mushroom and Ham Chowder 62

47. New Potatoes, Turkey and Kale Stew 63

48. Turkey Cocktail Meatballs ... 64

49. Rich Cheese and Meat Dip 65

50. Thanksgiving Turkey with Fruit 66

51. Lime Turkey Breasts 67

52. Hash Browns with Turkey Bacon 68

53. Turkey and Habanero Dip 69

54. Delicious Velveeta and Turkey Dip 70

55. Turkey with Chickpeas and Veggies 71

PORK 72

56. Saucy Pork Chops with Apricots 73

57. Soft Pork Tenderloin with Apples 74

58. Pork with Spinach, Apple and Pear 75

59. Cheese and Bacon Dip 76

60. Pork and Bacon with Mango Sauce................................77

61. Smoky Spare Ribs 78

62. Hash Brown Breakfast Casserole with Bacon 79

63. Pork Tenderloin with Vermouth Sauce........................... 80

64. Saucy Pork Ribs 81

65. Sautéed Pork Sausage with Sauerkraut 82

66. Super Yummy Pork Sausage Pie.................................. 83

67. Ham and Bean Soup with Kale 84

68. French-Style Lentil Soup 85

69. Easy Sausage and Velveeta Dip 86

70. Pork Strips with Pineapple .. 87

BEEF 88

71. Easy Sunday Beef Sandwiches 89
72. Cheesy Corn and Beef 90
73. Spiced Beef and Pork with Vegetables 91
74. Chipotle Beef and Pork Chili 92
75. Beer-Braised Chuck Roast 93
76. BBQ Pork and Beef Stew 94
77. Saucy Cocktail Meatballs 95
78. Ricotta and Beef Dip 96
79. Hot Mexican-Style Beef Dip .. 97
80. Barbecued Beef and Bean Soup 98
81. Festive Beef Meatballs 99
82. Sunday Hamburger Dip 100
83. The Best Christmas Steak Ever 101
84. Cheesy Beef with Sweet Corn 102
85. Dinner Beef and Pork Chili 103
86. Beef and Zucchini Loaf 104
87. Smoky Beef Chili 105
88. Christmas Dinner Beef Roast 106
89. Beef Roast with Mushrooms and Leeks 107
90. Meatballs in Barbecue Sauce 108

FISH & SEAFOOD 109

91. Baby Potato and Seafood Stew 110
92. Seafood and Tomato Chowder 111
93. Crab and Mayo Dip 112
94. Shrimp, Peppers, and Cheese Dip 113
95. Tomato and Seafood Stew 114
96. Potato, Corn and Shrimp Chowder 115
97. Shrimp with Potato and Corn 116
98. Salmon and Zucchini Soup .. 117
99. Tilapia Fillets with Kale 118
100. Shrimp and Corn Chowder 119

VEGAN 120

101. Vegan Sweet Farro 121
102. Vegan Miso Soup 122
103. Vegan Apple and Pear Pudding 123
104. Powerful Wheat Berry Breakfast 124
105. Multigrain Cereal with Golden Raisins 125
106. Morning Quinoa with Berries 126
107. Aromatic Fig Spread 127
108. Winter Vegetable Chowder 128
109. Cannellini Beans with Porcini Mushrooms 129

110. Sunrise Family Farro 130

111. Light Potato and Leek Purée 131

112. Easy Squash Chili 132

113. Summer Bean Salad with Peppers 133

114. Tangy Red Cabbage 134

115. Rich and Flavorful Three-Bean Chili with Corn 135

FAST SNACKS & APPETIZERS 136

116. Easy Boiled Peanuts 137

117. Classic Caramel Fondue 138

118. Broccoli and Water Chestnut Dip 139

119. Candied Coconut Banana ... 140

120. Apple and Mustard Cocktail Kielbasa 141

121. The Best Spiced Cashews Ever 142

122. Curry Pepper Almonds 143

123. Curried Cheese and Cranberry Dip 144

124. Candied Mixed Nuts 145

125. Cheesy Artichoke and Spinach Dipping Sauce 146

BEANS & GRAINS 147

126. Light and Aromatic Breakfast Risotto 148

127. Classic Grits with Swiss Cheese 149

128. Autumn Harvest Oatmeal 150

129. Habanero Turkey Chili 151

130. Overnight Oatmeal with Dried Cherries 152

131. Slow Cooker Muesli Mix 153

132. Nutty Overnight Porridge .. 154

133. Muesli with Black Currants and Seeds 155

134. Grandma's Butter Cornbread 156

135. Dinner Turkey Chili 157

DESSERTS 158

136. Every Day Cashew Banana Foster 159

137. Light and Easy Pumpkin Pie 160

138. Aunt's Two-Chocolate Fudge 161

139. Brownie Pudding Cake 162

140. Chocolate Nut Clusters 163

141. Apple and Apricot Crumble. 164

142. Peach and Sweet Potato Pudding 165

143. Coconut Hot Chocolate 166

144. Winter Hazelnut Fudge Sauce 167

145. Easy Berry Cobbler 168

146. Coconut Rice Pudding with Prunes 169

147. Vanilla Orange Custard 170

148. Delectable Crème Brûlée 171

149. Mom's Secret Chocolate Cake 172

150. Autumn Pear-Apple Cobbler with Prunes 173

INTRODUCTION

Isn't it just great that we can relax finally and have more time for ourselves and our families? Nobody wants to stand all day doing chores, cooking and doing the dishes. On the other hand, everybody likes a delicious food!

Luckily, new technology enables us to eat healthier and better while enjoying holidays, family gatherings, and everyday things that make us smile. There is an ingenious invention called "Slow cooker"!

GRANDMA KNOWS BEST

Technically speaking, the idea of slow cooking is not an invention of modern society. As a matter of fact, since ancient times, since the discovery of fire, people have used numerous slow cooking methods of food preparation. Most of us can remember a grandma's kitchen and invoke wonderful memories of her amazing home-cooked meals such as the beef stew, chicken soup, ground beef chili, or pork roast with gravy and mashed potatoes. This recipe collection enables you to prepare all of these old-fashioned recipes in an easy and fun way. We will reveal secrets of grandma's kitchen while learning to cook much better and cheaper. Here are a few tricks our grandmothers taught us:

A clever way to eat well on a tight budget.

As you probably already know, you can make budget-friendly meals easily and effortlessly if you have the right tool. You can buy the fattiest cuts of steak and turn them into delicious family meals. Just throw a nice combination of ingredients in your slow cooker, set the timer and let your electric "friend" cook it for you. This is one of the greatest advantages of slow cooking. If you want to stay within your budget, you should consider using a tough meat and poultry, cheap fish, hard and fibrous vegetables, chicken thighs, bone-in pork chops, pork ribs and other cheap cuts of meat. However, you have to use the right method of cooking for the desired results. With your slow cooker and a little skillfulness, your cheap cuts of meat don't dry out and they will come out so tender and delicious. Why does anyone have to spend hard-earned money on some expansive food when we can get the same results with the slow cooker?

Furthermore, you might be able to reduce energy use. Without a doubt, electric ovens and stoves consume a lot of electricity. Slow cooking is an energy-efficient way of cooking.

It has never been easier to eat healthy.

Doubtless, every person, regardless of age, must have a balanced diet. Your organism must be supplied with good and healthy food, as the material needed for its proper body and mind development, as well as a working power. Cooking at home is the best way to take control of your diet. In your slow cooker, you will use mainly fresh food and simmer it at a low temperature. It means that nutrition-rich ingredients from food are retained.

The most of the recipes in this book calls for legumes, vegetables, and high-fiber foods; then, you can prepare a tender meat full of juices without adding any oil or butter. You can prepare superfoods like oatmeal for breakfast or the porridge with seeds for a powerful and healthy post-workout dinner. People agree that cooking in a constantly moving environment of liquid brings the best results. Afterward, the slow cooker is a fully covered device so the nutrients have no chance to disappear; consequently, the vitamins and minerals are preserved.

The secret to getting more leisure time.

Your slow cooker is a time saving appliance so you can say goodbye to wasting your precious time in the kitchen. There is no special pre-preparation for this method of cooking. You can simply dump all ingredients, from vegetables and meat to shortening and a nice seasoning blend, in your cooker, and set the timer. After that, you can go to bed or wherever you want. When you get back home, the meal is ready. This is one of the greatest benefits of using the slow cooker – you can leave your cooker alone, without stirring and checking the contents.

However, if you are not in a hurry, it would be great if you could sear the meat or sauté the vegetables before slow cooking. This is one of the biggest grandma's secrets – if you find some time to sauté the onions and garlic in the skillet, the meal will be more flavorful, richer and tastier.

Simply follow these easy-to-prepare recipes and you will enjoy tempting fresh meals all day every day. Ultimately, the slow cooker is getting back to a simple way of life. Like the good old days when people spent more time socializing and having fun.

USING YOUR SLOW COOKER

You can make home cooking a breeze with the slow cooker in your kitchen. However, for maximum success, you should keep in mind a few basic rules:

1. First and foremost, reading manufacturer's instructions for operation and cleaning is a must.
2. Keep a lid on it. It is not necessary to lift the lid because you don't have to stir or check your meals, unless the recipe calls for it. In order to prevent meals, such as casseroles from sticking, you can use a slow-cooker liner or a nonstick cooking spray.
3. Then, be careful with seafood; it doesn't take long to cook. You can put it during the final 30 to 40 minutes of cooking.
4. Liquids do not evaporate during cooking in the slow cooker. Avoid adding too much water; use broth, vinegar, fruit juices, or wine instead.

This recipe collection is chock full of the best slow cooker recipes ever. It contains one hundred fifty recipes for the slow cooker that are separated into 10 basic categories: Vegetables & Side Dishes, Chicken, Turkey, Pork, Beef, Fish & Seafood, Vegan, Fast snacks, Beans & Grains and Desserts. You will be able to make a wide variety of meat and meatless recipes, without being a skilled kitchen professional.

PANTRY STAPLES FOR BETTER COOKING

If you are planning to make the most out of your slow cooker, a well-stocked pantry is a must! One of the best ways to save money, time, and energy in the kitchen is to have a good supply of essential ingredients in your pantry. Below is the list of the items that will help you create the best possible meals in your slow cooker.

Fresh food / Try to use fresh fruits and vegetables as much as you can. Add tender vegetables, such as green beans, sweet corn or snow peas, to the cooker during the final hour of cooking. Make sure that the vegetables are cut in uniform chunks. Do not forget to purchase fresh garlic, onions and leeks because they are irreplaceable and flavor-boosting ingredients. It is important to look for onions and shallots that are firm to the touch. Sautéing the onion and garlic in a small amount of oil is the best way to enhance the flavor of the entire meal. Sometimes, long-stewing can't produce desired results without all necessary steps and there are no shortcuts.

Dried beans and lentils / When it comes to the slow cooking, this is one of the greatest staples. You can make chilies, Mexican recipes, casseroles, and other old-fashioned meals.

Stock and broth / Beef, chicken, turkey, vegetable, and roasted-vegetable stocks, homemade or store-bought, powder or cubes, just pick what appeals to your taste. Dry packet soups are also handy here.

Cheese / Surely it is super versatile food so you can use it in numerous ways.

Seasonings / In terms of a well-stocked pantry, make sure to purchase fresh herbs and spice blends. For the flavorsome slow cooker meals, you can buy bulk herbs, fresh and dried, such as cilantro, parsley, rosemary, mint, thyme, sage, dill weed, and so on. When it comes to dried herbs, it is suggested to sauté them before adding them to the slow cooker.

Sauces / You can master slow cooking skills by using sauces such as BBQ, hoisin, tomato, Worcestershire, soy, sweet chili, etc.

For the best results, there are many other items such as canned tomatoes, coconut milk, plain flour, pasta, rice, vinegar, dried Parmesan, sugar, honey, wine, noodles, and so on.

All these recipes are designed to help you create delicious and homemade restaurant-quality meals for you, your guests, and your family. Each recipe is accompanied by information about cooking time, so you will be able to plan your day. Furthermore, this recipe collection is full of handy tricks and tips, such as serving ideas, information for substitutions, necessary kitchen equipment, etc. From now onwards, you will have a unique opportunity to experiment in your kitchen and make a wide variety of meals using only one clever kitchen appliance called "Slow Cooker". Bon appétit!

VEGETABLES & SIDE DISHES

– VEGETABLES & SIDE DISHES –

1. Mushroom and Kale Breakfast Quiche

Here is an effective, rich breakfast full of valuable nutrients. Serve with a spoonful of Greek-style yogurt. Enjoy!

Ready in about
2 hours
40 minutes

NUTRITIONAL INFORMATION
(Per Serving)

240 - Calories
12.1g - Fat
18.9g - Carbs
15g - Protein
7.8g - Sugars

Ingredients

- 2 slices bread, cubed
- 1/2 teaspoon garlic, finely minced
- Nonstick cooking spray
- 2 eggs
- 2 ounces mushrooms, chopped
- 1 scallion, chopped
- 4 ounces kale leaves, chopped
- 1/2 cup fat-free evaporated milk
- 2 tablespoons Cheddar cheese, shredded
- 1/4 teaspoon ground black pepper
- 1/2 teaspoon sea salt

Directions

1. Brush your slow cooker with a nonstick cooking spray. In a small-sized mixing dish, whisk the milk, eggs, and Cheddar cheese. Whisk to combine well.
2. Then, stir in the kale, mushrooms, garlic, and scallions. Season with salt and black pepper.
3. Place the bread cubes in one layer on the bottom of the slow cooker. Pour the milk-egg mixture over the top.
4. Cook, covered, on High for 2 hours 30 minutes or until the edges begin to pull away from the sides of your cooker. Serve warm.

– VEGETABLES & SIDE DISHES –

2. Sunrise Cremini Mushrooms

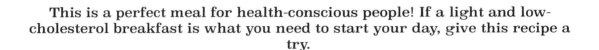

This is a perfect meal for health-conscious people! If a light and low-cholesterol breakfast is what you need to start your day, give this recipe a try.

Ready in about
7 hours
40 minutes

NUTRITIONAL
INFORMATION
(Per Serving)

52 - Calories
1g - Fat
4.8g - Carbs
4.4g - Protein
1.2g - Sugars

Ingredients
- 1/2 cup vegetable broth
- 1 teaspoon dried oregano
- 1/2 cayenne pepper
- 4 ounces cremini mushrooms, sliced
- 1/2 teaspoon salt
- 1/2 teaspoon dried basil
- 1/4 teaspoon black pepper, or more to taste
- 1 tablespoon white wine

Directions
1. Place all of the above ingredients in your slow cooker.
2. Cover with the lid; cook for 7 hours 30 minutes on Low heat setting. You can thicken the juices with cornstarch, if desired.
3. Serve with your favorite toasted bread. Bon appétit!

— VEGETABLES & SIDE DISHES —

3. Breakfast Hash Brown Casserole

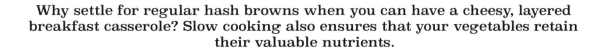

Why settle for regular hash browns when you can have a cheesy, layered breakfast casserole? Slow cooking also ensures that your vegetables retain their valuable nutrients.

Ready in about
11 hours
20 minutes

NUTRITIONAL
INFORMATION
(Per Serving)

430 - Calories
28.7g - Fat
15g - Carbs
30.9g - Protein
7g - Sugars

Ingredients

- 1 cup Colby cheese, shredded
- 1 teaspoon cayenne pepper
- 1/4 teaspoon ground black pepper
- 1/4 teaspoon dried dill weed
- 1 teaspoon sea salt
- 1/2 cup onions, diced
- 8 ounces bagged hash brown potatoes, frozen
- 1/2 cup milk
- 4 whole eggs
- 1/2 pound mushrooms, sliced

Directions

1. Arrange the ingredients in your slow cooker in this order: 1/2 of the potatoes, 1/2 of the onions, 1/2 of the mushroom, and 1/2 of the cheese.
2. Repeat the layers one more time.
3. In a measuring cup, beat the milk, eggs, dill weed, cayenne pepper, salt, and ground black pepper. Pour this mixture over the whole casserole.
4. Cook on Low for 11 hours. Serve warm.

– VEGETABLES & SIDE DISHES –

4. Sunday Morning Asparagus Casserole

Every home cook has their own secret ingredient to the casserole. What is your favorite recipe ingredient for this amazing vegetarian lunch?

Ready in about
5 hours
10 minutes

NUTRITIONAL INFORMATION
(Per Serving)

171 - Calories
10.6g - Fat
10.9g - Carbs
8.8g - Protein
1.7g - Sugars

Ingredients

- 1 hard-boiled egg, sliced
- 4 ounces cream of mushroom soup
- 6 saltines, coarsely crushed
- 4 ounces asparagus, drained and sliced
- 1/2 teaspoon butter, softened
- 1/4 cup Cheddar cheese, grated

Directions

1. Place the asparagus in a lightly-buttered slow cooker baking insert. Then, whisk the cream of mushroom soup with Cheddar cheese.
2. Top the asparagus with sliced eggs; pour in the soup mixture. Top with the cracker crumbs. Dot with softened butter. Cover and cook for 5 hours on Low. Enjoy!

– VEGETABLES & SIDE DISHES –

5. Barley with Mushrooms and Scallions

Barley is a versatile cereal grain that is rich in vitamins, minerals, dietary fiber, and antioxidants. Its nutty and pleasant flavor adds complexity to any vegetable meal.

Ready in about
4 hours
10 minutes

NUTRITIONAL
INFORMATION
(Per Serving)

212 - Calories
3.8g - Fat
37.4g - Carbs
9.7g - Protein
2g - Sugars

Ingredients

- 1 teaspoon butter
- 2 scallions, chopped
- 4 ounces button mushrooms, sliced
- 1/4 teaspoon ground black pepper, or more to your liking
- 1/4 teaspoon seasoned salt
- 1/2 teaspoon cayenne pepper
- 3/4 cup chicken broth
- 1/2 cup barley

Directions

1. Combine all ingredients in your slow cooker. Stir until everything is well mixed.
2. Cover the cooker; cook on Low heat setting for 4 hours.
3. Serve right away with sour cream or tomato ketchup, if desired. Enjoy!

– VEGETABLES & SIDE DISHES –

6. Lentil, Kale and Sweet Potato Soup

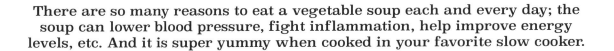

There are so many reasons to eat a vegetable soup each and every day; the soup can lower blood pressure, fight inflammation, help improve energy levels, etc. And it is super yummy when cooked in your favorite slow cooker.

Ready in about 8 hours

NUTRITIONAL INFORMATION
(Per Serving)

279 - Calories
2.7g - Fat
47.1g - Carbs
17.1g - Protein
11.2g - Sugars

Ingredients

- 1/4 cup green lentils, soaked
- 1 sweet potato, diced
- 1 clove garlic, finely minced
- 1/4 teaspoon freshly ground black pepper, to taste
- 1/4 teaspoon salt
- 1/2 tablespoon fresh rosemary, finely minced
- 1/2 medium-sized parsnip, finely chopped
- 1 small-sized carrot, sliced
- 1/2 teaspoon adobo sauce
- 1/2 cup red onions, diced
- 1 cup kale, torn into pieces
- 1/2 cup celery stalk, finely chopped
- 3 cups vegetable broth

Directions

1. Place all ingredients, except for kale, in your slow cooker.
2. Slow cook for 7 hours 30 minutes on Low.
3. Once the time is up, stir in the kale. Stir well to combine.
4. Taste, adjust the seasonings, and cook, uncovered, for another 15 minutes. Serve immediately. Bon appétit!

– VEGETABLES & SIDE DISHES –

7. Cauliflower and Quinoa Soup

Any sort of sweet potato will work in this hearty soup. Our aim is to make a colorful and chunky soup that is both healthy and appealing. Serve with croutons.

Ready in about
5 hours
40 minutes

NUTRITIONAL INFORMATION
(Per Serving)

324 - Calories
9.6g - Fat
50g - Carbs
12.1g - Protein
6.7g - Sugars

Ingredients

- 1 ½ cups water
- 2 sweet potatoes, diced
- 1/4 cup quinoa
- 2 cloves garlic, finely minced
- 1 ½ cups vegetable broth
- 1 teaspoon dried basil
- 1/4 teaspoon ground black pepper
- 1/4 teaspoon dried dill weed
- 1/2 teaspoon dried marjoram
- 1/2 teaspoon salt
- 1/2 teaspoon dried oregano
- 1 tablespoon oil
- 1 cup spinach, torn into small pieces
- 1/2 small-sized head cauliflowers florets
- 1 small-sized onion, finely chopped

Directions

1. Heat the oil in your slow cooker; then, sauté the onion with garlic for 5 minutes or until tender, fragrant, and translucent.
2. Then, stir in the rest of the ingredients, except for the spinach. Slow cook for 5 hours on Low.
3. Lastly, stir in the spinach; cook for 20 minutes longer and serve hot.

— VEGETABLES & SIDE DISHES —

8. Harvest Butternut Squash Stew

A one-pot meal is the perfect solution for your lazy Sunday. Feel free to use another combo of seasonings according to your personal preferences. Enjoy!

Ready in about
5 hours
15 minutes

NUTRITIONAL INFORMATION
(Per Serving)

283 - Calories
7.8g - Fat
5.2g - Carbs
5.3g - Protein
10.7g - Sugars

Ingredients

- 1/2 pound butternut squash, diced
- 1/2 pound potatoes, diced
- 1/2 tablespoon apple cider vinegar
- 1/2 teaspoon salt
- 1/2 teaspoon celery seeds
- 1/4 teaspoon ground black pepper, to taste
- 1/2 teaspoon fennel seeds
- 1/2 teaspoon cayenne pepper
- 1/2 teaspoon smoked paprika
- 1 parsnip, chopped
- 1 carrot, thinly sliced
- 1 celery stalk, chopped
- 1 tablespoon vegetable oil
- 1 cup vegetable stock
- 1/2 cup tomato purée
- 2 cloves garlic, finely minced
- 1 bay leaf
- 4-5 black peppercorns
- 1/2 onion, chopped

Directions

1. First of all, warm vegetable oil in your slow cooker over medium heat. Now, sauté all veggies until just tender, about 9 minutes.
2. Throw in the rest of the above items; put on the lid and cook the mixture on Low heat settings for 5 hours.
3. Serve warm with your favorite crusty bread. Bon appétit!

– VEGETABLES & SIDE DISHES –

9. Aunt's Broccoli and Quinoa Soup

This is a versatile soup so you can add your favorite vegetables and seasonings to boost this basic recipe. Serve with pull-apart cheese bread and delight your party guests.

Ready in about 6 hours

NUTRITIONAL INFORMATION (Per Serving)

375 - Calories
4.9g - Fat
7.6g - Carbs
9.8g - Protein
3.6g - Sugars

Ingredients

- 1/3 cup quinoa
- 1 cup broccoli florets
- 1 cup water
- 1 ½ cups vegetable stock
- 2 cloves garlic, finely minced
- 1/4 teaspoon dried basil
- 1/4 teaspoon ground black pepper, to your liking
- 1/4 teaspoon dried dill weed
- 1/4 teaspoon fennel seeds
- 1 teaspoon dried oregano
- 1 teaspoon cayenne pepper
- 1/2 teaspoon salt
- 1 sprig dried thyme
- 1 tablespoon canola oil
- 1 cup kale, torn into small pieces
- 1 small-sized leeks, finely chopped
- 2 sweet potatoes, diced

Directions

1. First, warm canola oil in your slow cooker over medium heat; then, sauté the leeks and garlic for 5 minutes or until fragrant.
2. Then, stir in the remaining items, except the kale. Slow cook for 5 hours 30 minutes on Low heat setting.
3. Afterwards, stir in the kale; cook for 20 minutes more; serve warm. Enjoy!

— VEGETABLES & SIDE DISHES —

10. The Best Pumpkin Bisque Ever

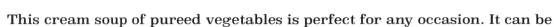

This cream soup of pureed vegetables is perfect for any occasion. It can be served as a complete meal, vegetarian main course, or starter. It's up to you!

Ready in about
7 hours
15 minutes

NUTRITIONAL
INFORMATION
(Per Serving)

135 - Calories
5.2g - Fat
18.3g - Carbs
6.1g - Protein
10.8g - Sugars

Ingredients

- 1 cup pumpkin, puréed
- 1/4 teaspoon white pepper
- 1/2 tablespoon sage
- 1/4 teaspoon kosher salt, or more to taste
- 1/2 cup fat-free evaporated milk
- 2 scallions, chopped
- 2 cups water
- 1 clove garlic, minced

Directions

1. Simply drop all of the above ingredients into your slow cooker. Give it a good stir.
2. Cook, covered, on Low heat setting for 7 hours.
3. Then, blend the bisque using an immersion blender.
4. Divide your bisque among individual soup bowls. Add a few sprinkles of pumpkin pie spice, if desired. Enjoy!

– VEGETABLES & SIDE DISHES –

11. Easy Curried Cauliflower Soup

This is the soup that your family will love for sure! Curry powder adds a deep and earthy flavor to this unique dish.

Ready in about
7 hours
40 minutes

NUTRITIONAL INFORMATION
(Per Serving)

46 - Calories
0.1g - Fat
8.5g - Carbs
4.4g - Protein
3.6g - Sugars

Ingredients

- 1/2 cup water
- 1/4 teaspoon celery seeds
- 1/2 tablespoon curry powder
- 1 teaspoon cumin
- 1 clove garlic, minced
- 1 cup chicken stock
- 1/2 head cauliflower, broken into florets
- 1/2 cup yellow onion, minced

Directions

1. Put the ingredients into your slow cooker. Stir till everything is well combined.
2. Cook for 7 hours 30 minutes on Low heat setting.
3. Purée the soup using an immersion blender and serve warm. Divide the mixture among individual soup bowls. Enjoy!

– VEGETABLES & SIDE DISHES –

12. Potato and Carrot Potage

Just like a soup, a bowl of potage has a lot of health benefits. Vegetable potage is packed with valuable nutrients. It is low in calorie and good for weight loss. On the other hand, good potage can make you energized for hours.

Servings 6

Ready in about
6 hours
15 minutes

NUTRITIONAL
INFORMATION
(Per Serving)

108 - Calories
0.2g - Fat
24.8g - Carbs
3.3g - Protein
3.5g - Sugars

Ingredients

- 1 russet potato, peeled and cubed
- 1/2 teaspoon kosher salt
- 1/4 teaspoon ground black pepper
- 1 clove garlic, minced
- 1 carrot, diced
- 2 cups water
- 1 cup scallions, chopped

Directions

1. Put all ingredients into the slow cooker. Cook on Low setting for 6 hours.
2. Purée the mixture using an immersion blender. Serve hot.

– VEGETABLES & SIDE DISHES –

13. Dilled Vegetable Soup

It's hard to imagine a really good lunch without a bowl of hearty vegetable soup. This Mediterranean inspired soup is both delicious and healthy!

Ready in about
7 hours
20 minutes

NUTRITIONAL INFORMATION
(Per Serving)

95 - Calories
0.7g - Fat
20.9g - Carbs
3.1g - Protein
5.7g Sugars

Ingredients

- 1 ½ cups turkey stock
- 1 teaspoon minced garlic
- 1/4 cup canned diced tomatoes
- 1/2 cup carrots, diced
- 1/2 parsnip, diced
- 1/2 cup shallots, minced
- 1/2 cup celery stalk, diced
- 1/2 teaspoon ground black pepper
- 1/2 tablespoon fresh dill
- 2 sprigs dried rosemary, crushed
- 1 sprig dried thyme, crushed
- 1/3 teaspoon sea salt
- 1/2 cup turnip, diced

Directions

1. Simply drop all of the above ingredients in your slow cooker; stir vigorously.
2. Cook for 7 hours on Low heat setting. Divide the soup among two individual bowls.
3. Sprinkle with some extra dill weed and garnish with a dollop of sour cream, if desired.

― VEGETABLES & SIDE DISHES ―

14. Hot Mixed Vegetable Stew

Is there anything better than rich, warm vegetable stew during winter weekdays? Serve this hearty stew with wild rice or pasta.

Ready in about
3 hours
40 minutes

NUTRITIONAL INFORMATION
(Per Serving)

255 - Calories
14.6g - Fat
28.9g - Carbs
4.4g - Protein
7g - Sugars

Ingredients

- 1 tablespoon olive oil
- 1 cup sliced yellow squash
- 1 clove garlic, crushed
- 1/2 cup bell peppers, chopped
- 1/4 cup diced okra
- 1/2 cup fresh corn kernels
- 1/2 habanero pepper, seeded and finely minced
- 1/4 teaspoon salt
- 1/2 tablespoon fresh thyme, minced
- 1/3 teaspoon black pepper
- 1 tablespoon lemon juice
- 1/2 cup red onions, thinly sliced
- 1 cup zucchini, sliced

Directions

1. On the bottom of your slow cooker, place the onions and garlic, followed by yellow squash, bell pepper, habanero pepper, zucchini, thyme, and lemon juice.
2. Drizzle olive oil over the top and season with salt and ground black pepper. Cook on Low for 3 hours.
3. Stir in the okra and corn. Cook on High for an additional 30 minutes, stirring occasionally. Serve hot and enjoy!

— VEGETABLES & SIDE DISHES —

15. Light Saucy Eggplant

Anchovy paste is a versatile ingredient that can enhance flavor in everything, from vegetables to meat and seafood. It is made from anchovy fillets, vinegar, olive oil, and sugar.

Ready in about
2 hours
40 minutes

NUTRITIONAL
INFORMATION
(Per Serving)

66 - Calories
3.5g - Fat
7.5g - Carbs
2.8g - Protein
3.4g - Sugars

Ingredients

- 1/2 pound eggplant, peeled and cubed
- 1/2 tablespoon tahini
- 1 tablespoon anchovy paste
- 1/2 teaspoon kosher salt, or more to taste
- 1/8 teaspoon freshly cracked black pepper
- 1 tablespoon water

Directions

1. Place the water, anchovy paste, and tahini in your slow cooker. Stir to dissolve the anchovy paste.
2. Stir in the eggplant and toss to coat. Season with ground black pepper and kosher salt.
3. Cook on High setting for 2 hours 30 minutes. Serve and enjoy!

– VEGETABLES & SIDE DISHES –

16. Hot Stuffed Peppers with Cauliflower

You don't have to heat up your whole stove top and oven for cooking stuffed peppers. You can get even better peppers in your slow cooker.

**Ready in about
5 hours
40 minutes**

**NUTRITIONAL
INFORMATION
(Per Serving)**

228 - Calories
0.5g - Fat
51.6g - Carbs
6g - Protein
8.8g - Sugars

Ingredients

- 1/4 cup water
- 6 ounces canned fire-roasted diced tomatoes with garlic
- 1/2 teaspoon hot Mexican chili powder
- 3/4 cup cauliflower florets
- 1/2 teaspoon freshly ground black pepper
- 1/4 teaspoon kosher salt
- 1/2 cup onions, thinly sliced
- 1 red bell pepper, seeded and thinly sliced
- 1 green bell pepper, seeded and thinly sliced
- 1/2 cup jasmine rice

Directions

1. Lay the peppers on the bottom of your slow cooker.
2. Then, to make the filling, combine the remaining ingredients, except the water; stir to combine well.
3. Stuff the peppers. Add the water. Cook on Low setting for 5 hours 30 minutes. Enjoy!

– VEGETABLES & SIDE DISHES –

17. Pepper and Hominy Stew

This plant-based stew is the perfect meal for those people who follow a vegan diet. Sure, you don't need to be vegan to enjoy this amazing meal – it can easily fit into your weight-loss plan, too. You can get creative and add your favorite spices like cumin or bay leaf powder.

Ready in about
7 hours
40 minutes

NUTRITIONAL INFORMATION
(Per Serving)

161 - Calories
2.9g - Fat
31.1g - Carbs
4.6g - Protein
7.7g - Sugars

Ingredients

- 1 zucchini, diced
- 1 Serrano pepper, diced
- 2 cloves garlic, minced
- 1 jalapeño pepper, diced
- 1/2 yellow onion, diced
- 2 cups water
- 10 ounces canned hominy
- 1/2 teaspoon kosher salt
- 1/2 teaspoon black pepper, freshly ground
- 1/2 teaspoon olive oil
- 1/2 cup tomatoes, chopped
- 2 ounces canned green peppers, diced

Directions

1. Heat the oil in a pan over medium heat. Then, sauté the onions and garlic until just tender. Now, add all peppers and continue sautéing until fragrant and tender.
2. Add the onion-pepper mixture to the slow cooker. Add the water, tomato, hominy, kosher salt, and black pepper. Stir to combine well. Cook for 6 hours on Low.
3. Stir in the zucchini; cook on High setting for 1 hour 30 minutes longer. Stir prior to serving.

— VEGETABLES & SIDE DISHES —

18. Rainbow Mushroom Soup

Mushrooms, peppers and cauliflower are all cooked together in this rich soup for an appetizing lunch. You can substitute button mushrooms for cremini mushrooms as well. Bon appétit!

Ready in about
5 hours
40 minutes

NUTRITIONAL INFORMATION
(Per Serving)

201 - Calories
1.4g - Fat
42.9g - Carbs
8.4g - Protein
16.3g - Sugars

Ingredients

- 1/2 head cauliflower, broken into florets
- 1/2 cup turnip, chopped
- 1 potato, diced
- 1 sprig fresh thyme, finely minced
- 1 tablespoon fresh parsley, finely chopped
- 1/2 tablespoon fresh cilantro, finely chopped
- 1 carrot, sliced
- 1/2 cup cremini mushrooms, sliced
- 1/2 cup canned roasted tomato
- 1/2 cup yellow squash, diced
- 1/2 medium-sized leek, diced
- 1 teaspoon sea salt
- 1/4 teaspoon freshly cracked black pepper, or more to taste
- 1/2 cup snow peas, frozen
- 2 cups chicken stock
- 2 tablespoons chopped green bell peppers
- 1/2 cup red bell peppers, diced

Directions

1. Simply combine all of the above ingredients in your slow cooker.
2. Then, slow cook for 5 hours 30 minutes or until the vegetables are tender.
3. After that, adjust the seasonings. Serve in individual bowls and enjoy!

– VEGETABLES & SIDE DISHES –

19. Baked Potato Appetizer

Cozy up to this old-fashion appetizer, made with fresh potatoes and great spices! Serve with enough salad and cream cheese.

Ready in about
9 hours
10 minutes

NUTRITIONAL INFORMATION
(Per Serving)

156 - Calories
0.2g - Fat
35.6g - Carbs
3.8g - Protein
2.6g - Sugars

Ingredients

- 1/2 teaspoon cayenne pepper
- 1 teaspoon salt
- 1/4 teaspoon ground black pepper, or more to taste
- 4 potatoes

Directions

1. First, prick your potatoes with a fork; then, wrap each potato in foil.
2. Add the potatoes to the slow cooker. Cover and cook on Low setting for 9 hours.
3. Season with salt, black pepper, and cayenne pepper.

— VEGETABLES & SIDE DISHES —

20. Bavarian Cabbage with Apples

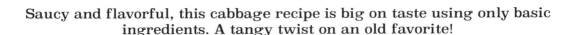

Saucy and flavorful, this cabbage recipe is big on taste using only basic ingredients. A tangy twist on an old favorite!

Ready in about
9 hours
15 minutes

NUTRITIONAL INFORMATION
(Per Serving)

317 - Calories
15.6g - Fat
44.6g - Carbs
3.3g - Protein
30.3g - Sugars

Ingredients

- 2 tablespoons bacon grease
- 1 garlic clove, minced
- 1/4 cup apple cider vinegar
- 1/2 cup onions, chopped
- 1/2 teaspoon salt
- 2 bay leaves
- 2 tart apples, cored and diced
- 1 cup hot water
- 1/2 head of cabbage, shredded
- 4-5 black peppercorns

Directions

1. Just throw all ingredients into the slow cooker in order listed above.
2. Cover and cook on Low for 9 hours.
3. Remove the cover, discard the bay leaves, and stir well before serving.

CHICKEN

– CHICKEN –

21. Chicken Chili Beans

A mild or spicy chili? You can adjust this recipe according to your taste. Simply reduce or increase the number of chilies.

Ready in about 6 hours

NUTRITIONAL INFORMATION
(Per Serving)

456 - Calories
12.2g - Fat
47.5g - Carbs
45.3g - Protein
14.1g - Sugars

Ingredients

- 5 ounces Northern beans
- 1/4 teaspoon cumin
- 2 ounces of green chilies, finely minced
- 1/2 teaspoon dried basil
- 1/2 teaspoon dry oregano
- 1/4 teaspoon sea salt
- 1/2 teaspoon dried dill weed
- 1/2 teaspoon smoked paprika
- 2 tablespoons milk
- 2 green onions, chopped
- 1 clove garlic, minced
- 1/2 pound chicken breasts
- 1 cup chicken broth
- 1 teaspoon fresh lime juice

Directions

1. Combine all of the above ingredients in your slow cooker. Cover and set the slow cooker to Low.
2. Then, slow cook for 5 hours 30 minutes.
3. After that, remove the chicken from the cooker; shred it with two forks; return it back to the cooker. Cook for another 20 minutes on Low. Serve warm.

– CHICKEN –

22. Tandoori-inspired Pulled Chicken

Actually, a tandoor is a cylindrical clay oven. This is a traditional way of cooking in the Indian subcontinent. You can achieve a great result in your slow cooker, too.

Ready in about
5 hours
15 minutes

NUTRITIONAL INFORMATION
(Per Serving)

346 - Calories
15g - Fat
5.4g - Carbs
45g - Protein
2.3g - Sugars

Ingredients

For the Pulled Chicken:
- 3/4 pound chicken breasts
- 2 cloves garlic, finely minced
- 1/4 teaspoon salt, or more to taste
- 1/4 teaspoon ground black pepper
- 1/2 cup onion, finely chopped
- 1 ½ cups chicken broth

For the Tandoori Sauce:
- Ground black pepper and salt, to taste
- 1/2 teaspoon turmeric
- 1/2 teaspoon cumin
- 1/2 teaspoon cayenne pepper
- 1/4 cup coconut milk

Directions

1. Bring the chicken broth to a boil in your slow cooker; then, stir in chicken, onion, garlic, black pepper and salt.
2. Seal the cooker; slow cook for 3 hours 30 minutes on Low. Once the time is up, remove the chicken from the cooker and pull it using a fork.
3. Then, whisk the sauce ingredients in a mixing dish. Add the sauce to the slow cooker; cook for 1 hour 30 minutes on Low.
4. Serve right away.

– CHICKEN –

23. Tangy Mesquite Chicken

It is so easy and convenient to cook the chicken in the slow cooker. It's like someone's making a meal for you!

Ready in about
5 hours
40 minutes

NUTRITIONAL INFORMATION
(Per Serving)

539 - Calories
10.4g - Fat
7.7g - Carbs
40.8g - Protein
50.8g - Sugars

Ingredients

- 1/2 bottle BBQ sauce
- 1/2 teaspoon mesquite seasoning
- 1 tablespoon white vinegar
- 1/2 teaspoon onion powder
- 1/4 teaspoon sea salt, or more to taste
- 1/2 teaspoon ground black pepper
- 1/2 teaspoon garlic powder
- 1/2 tablespoon honey
- 2 pieces boneless chicken breasts

Directions

1. In a bowl, mix all ingredients, except for chicken breasts. Let it marinate at least 30 minutes.
2. Lay the chicken in the slow cooker. Pour the marinade over the chicken. Slow cook for 5 hours.
3. Serve with coleslaw, if desired. Bon appétit!

– CHICKEN –

24. Party Chicken Wings with Honey and Ketchup

Here is a perfect recipe for Superbowl Sunday. Find some inspiration and make these sticky wings that will impress your friends!

Ready in about
7 hours
10 minutes

NUTRITIONAL INFORMATION
(Per Serving)

275 - Calories
12.1g - Fat
20.8g - Carbs
21.5g - Protein
19.3g - Sugars

Ingredients

- 1 tablespoon tomato ketchup
- 2 tablespoons soy sauce
- 1 tablespoon sesame oil
- 1/4 teaspoon crushed red pepper flakes, or more to taste
- 1/4 teaspoon cumin seeds
- 1/2 teaspoon garlic, finely minced
- 1/4 teaspoon sea salt
- 1/2 teaspoon shallot powder
- 2 tablespoons honey
- 1 pound chicken wings, tips discarded

Directions

1. First, cut each chicken wing into halves.
2. Then, make the sauce by mixing the remaining ingredients in a medium-sized bowl; mix till everything is well combined.
3. Arrange the wings on the bottom of your slow cooker; pour sauce over chicken wings. Cook 7 hours on Low setting.
4. Transfer them to the serving dish and sprinkle with fresh cilantro for serving. Enjoy!

— CHICKEN —

25. Cherry-Glazed Chicken Wings

Wings are endlessly inspiring, particularly if you cook them in your slow cooker. You can also try sprinkling in a pinch of paprika or chili powder.

Ready in about
5 hours
30 minutes

NUTRITIONAL INFORMATION
(Per Serving)

567 - Calories
13.3g - Fat
75.9g - Carbs
29.5g - Protein
54g - Sugars

Ingredients

- 1 tablespoon butter
- 1/2 teaspoon garlic powder
- 1/2 teaspoon ground black pepper
- 1/2 teaspoon salt, or more to taste
- 1/2 cup cherry preserves, preferably sour cherry
- 1 pound medium-sized chicken wings, cut up
- 1/2 tablespoon dark soy sauce

Directions

1. Brown chicken wings in a skillet for 15 minutes or until golden brown; transfer them to the slow cooker.
2. Now, add the remaining ingredients to the slow cooker.
3. Cook on Low setting for 5 hours or until cooked through. Serve warm and enjoy!

– CHICKEN –

26. Chicken with Jalapeño and Beans

Pressure cooked chicken and beans are awesome! This versatile meal goes well with winter squash, asparagus and sweet potatoes.

Ready in about 6 hours

NUTRITIONAL INFORMATION
(Per Serving)

374 - Calories
9.2g - Fat
31.8g - Carbs
39.6g - Protein
2g - Sugars

Ingredients

- 1 cup vegetable stock
- 5 ounces canned beans
- 1/4 teaspoon dried rosemary
- 1/2 teaspoon dried oregano
- 1 teaspoon cumin
- 1/4 teaspoon dried basil
- 1 jalapeño pepper, minced
- 1/2 cup shallots, finely chopped
- 2 tablespoons milk
- 1/2 tablespoon balsamic vinegar
- Sea salt and black pepper, to taste
- 1/2 pound chicken breasts
- 1 clove garlic, finely minced

Directions

1. Combine all ingredients in your slow cooker; stir until everything is well combined.
2. Then, cook for 5 hours 30 minutes on Low heat setting.
3. After that, remove the chicken from the cooker; shred it using two forks; add it back to the cooker. Cook the mixture for another 20 minutes on Low; serve hot.

– CHICKEN –

27. Moroccan-Style Tomato and Chicken Stew

A chicken stew is definitely one of the best options to make you luncheon a delicious pleasure. In this recipe, you can substitute Habanero peppers for Serrano peppers with the same result.

Ready in about
5 hours
15 minutes

NUTRITIONAL INFORMATION
(Per Serving)

462 - Calories
10.3g - Fat
57.2g - Carbs
36.9g - Protein
13.2g - Sugars

Ingredients

- 1/2 cup chicken broth
- 1/2 celery stalk, chopped
- 1/2 carrot, thinly sliced
- 1/2 Serrano pepper, thinly sliced
- 1 tomato, diced
- 1/2 cup onions, finely chopped
- 5 ounces of chickpeas
- 1/2 parsnip, chopped
- 1/3 teaspoon freshly cracked black pepper
- 1/4 teaspoon celery seeds
- 1/2 teaspoon cumin seeds
- 1/3 teaspoon sea salt
- 1/2 teaspoon fennel seeds
- 1 bay leaf
- 1/2 teaspoon whole black peppercorns
- 1 pound chicken thighs
- 1 tablespoon tomato paste

Directions

1. Simply drop all of the above ingredients in your slow cooker. Gently stir using a spoon.
2. Then, cook for 5 hours on Low heat setting.
3. Garnish with your favorite crusty bread. Serve it right away.

– CHICKEN –

28. Chicken, Orzo and Kale Soup

Preparing a chicken soup in the slow cooker is not only fun, it's also very simple. Chicken soup is a quite versatile dish so let your imagination run wild!

Ready in about 8 hours

NUTRITIONAL INFORMATION
(Per Serving)

136 - Calories
2g - Fat
19.4g - Carbs
10.4g - Protein
2.5g - Sugars

Ingredients

- 1/2 cooked chicken breast, cubed
- 1 clove garlic, minced
- Salt and ground black pepper, to taste
- 2 cups roasted vegetable stock
- 1/2 cup red onion, thinly sliced
- 2 cups fresh kale leaves
- 1/2 teaspoon ginger, grated
- 1 tablespoon lime juice
- 2 tablespoons orzo, dried

Directions

1. Add the garlic, lime juice, ginger, stock, and red onion to your slow cooker. Put on the lid and cook on Low approximately 7 hours.
2. Stir in the chicken cubes; turn the heat to High and cook for 35 minutes more.
3. Next, throw in the orzo and kale. Continue to cook for further 20 minutes on High.
4. Season with salt and black pepper. Stir before serving, adjust seasoning, and serve hot.

– CHICKEN –

29. Chicken and Root Vegetable Soup

This is an elegant and flavorsome chicken meal for the perfect family lunch. Serve this irresistible combination of chicken, chickpeas and vegetables in individual soup bowls with croutons.

Ready in about
7 hours
30 minutes

NUTRITIONAL INFORMATION
(Per Serving)

517 - Calories
10.1g - Fat
69.7g - Carbs
40.8g - Protein
23.7g - Sugars

Ingredients

- 1 cup cooked chicken, cut into bite-sized chunks
- 1/2 teaspoon olive oil
- 5 ounces canned chickpeas, drained
- 1 carrot, diced
- 1/4 cup turnip, chopped
- 2 cups vegetable broth
- 1/2 onion, diced
- 2 ounces canned green chilies
- 1/2 parsnip, diced

Directions

1. Heat the oil in a skillet over medium flame. Sauté the onions, parsnip, turnip, and carrots until they're are slightly softened.
2. Then, add the remaining ingredients, except the chicken. Stir until everything is well combined. Add the mixture to the slow cooker and cook on Low heat setting up to 7 hours.
3. Afterwards, add the chicken and cook until thoroughly warmed. Serve hot and enjoy!

– CHICKEN –

30. Chicken Stew with Potatoes and Corn

This hearty chicken stew is both dinner-worthy and healthy lunch option. You will love this recipe, especially on autumn days.

Ready in about
8 hours
40 minutes

NUTRITIONAL INFORMATION
(Per Serving)

243 - Calories
7.3g - Fat
22g - Carbs
23.2g - Protein
4.6g - Sugars

Ingredients

- 1 cup boneless skinless chicken breast, cut into cubes
- 1 clove garlic, minced
- 1/2 cup potatoes, diced
- 1/2 cup chicken stock
- 1 tablespoon fresh rosemary, minced
- 1/2 onion, diced
- 1/2 tablespoon all-purpose flour
- Salt and black pepper, to taste
- 1/4 cup corn kernels, frozen or fresh
- 1/2 teaspoon olive oil
- 1 carrot, diced

Directions

1. Heat olive oil in a skillet over medium heat. Then, sauté the onions, flour, carrots, garlic, potatoes, rosemary, and chicken.
2. Now, transfer sautéed ingredients to the slow cooker. Sprinkle with salt and ground black pepper. Pour in the stock and stir to combine. Cook on Low for 8 hours.
3. Add the corn kernels. Cover and cook on High for 30 minutes longer. Give it a good stir and serve warm.

– CHICKEN –

31. Habanero Chicken Chili

The habanero is a variety of chili pepper. It is rich in vitamins, minerals, and dietary fiber. It may prevent cancer and cardiovascular diseases.

Ready in about
9 hours
15 minutes

NUTRITIONAL
INFORMATION
(Per Serving)

446 - Calories
3.5g - Fat
62.9g - Carbs
42.5g - Protein
5.3g - Sugars

Ingredients

- 8 ounces canned kidney beans, drained and rinsed
- 1/2 teaspoon chipotle, finely minced
- 1 clove garlic, chopped
- 1 chipotle chili in adobo
- 1/2 tablespoon habanero hot sauce
- 1/3 teaspoon freshly ground black pepper
- 1/2 teaspoon cayenne
- 1 teaspoon sea salt, to taste
- 1 cup chicken, ground
- 1/2 teaspoon liquid smoke
- 2 scallions, chopped
- 8 ounces canned diced tomatoes

Directions

1. First, sauté the chicken in a skillet until just cooked through. Drain the excess fat and transfer the sautéed chicken to the slow cooker.
2. Add all of the above ingredients to the slow cooker.
3. Give it a good stir. Cook on Low for 9 hours. Bon appétit!

– CHICKEN –

32. Old-Fashioned Roasted Chicken with Vegetables

This chicken dish is not only easy to cook, but it is full of valuable nutrients as well. It is loaded with fresh vegetables and looks beautiful on your dining table.

Ready in about
7 hours
20 minutes

NUTRITIONAL
INFORMATION
(Per Serving)

289 - Calories
2.4g - Fat
42.1g - Carbs
24.8g - Protein
6.3g - Sugars

Ingredients

- 1 cup chicken
- 1/2 teaspoon liquid smoke
- 1/2 teaspoon sea salt
- 1/2 teaspoon ground black pepper
- 1/4 teaspoon smoked paprika
- 2 large-sized potatoes, halved
- 1 large-sized parsnip, cut into matchsticks
- 1 carrot, cut into matchsticks
- 1 bay leaf
- 1 onion, thinly sliced

Directions

1. Cover the bottom of your slow cooker with 1/2 of the sliced onions.
2. Then, lay the chicken on top of the onions. Top the chicken with the remaining sliced onions.
3. Scatter the carrots, potatoes and parsnips around the chicken. Generously season with salt, ground black pepper, and smoked paprika. Drizzle the liquid smoke over the meat. Afterwards, add the bay leaf.
4. Put on the lid and cook on Low heat setting for 7 hours. Discard the chicken skin before serving. Serve warm. Bon appétit!

– CHICKEN –

33. Easiest Barbecue Chicken Ever

This tender chicken can be served on any occasion. Don't forget to add a pinch of freshly grated nutmeg for some extra oomph!

Ready in about 5 hours

NUTRITIONAL INFORMATION
(Per Serving)

165 - Calories
2.3g - Fat
14.7g - Carbs
20.7g - Protein
13.7g - Sugars

Ingredients

- 2 tablespoons tomato ketchup
- Kosher salt and ground black pepper, to your liking
- 1 bay leaf
- 1/2 teaspoon cayenne pepper
- 1/2 teaspoon black peppercorns
- 1 tablespoon Worcestershire sauce
- 1 cup chicken, skin removed and cut up
- 2 tablespoons brown sugar

Directions

1. Lay your chicken on the bottom of the slow cooker. Add bay leaf and black peppercorns.
2. In a mixing dish, combine the remaining ingredients until everything is well incorporated. Then, pour the mixture over the chicken.
3. Cook 4 hours 30 minutes on High. Enjoy!

– CHICKEN –

34. Tangy 'n' Sweet Chicken Wings

This recipe showcases chicken wings at their finest. These wings are easy to make but they have a rich taste thanks to the mustard and Worcestershire sauce.

Ready in about
7 hours
40 minutes

NUTRITIONAL INFORMATION
(Per Serving)

305 - Calories
6.8g - Fat
39.3g - Carbs
21.8g - Protein
36.7g - Sugars

Ingredients

- 1 tablespoon mild mustard
- 1/2 cup brown sugar
- 1/2 teaspoon celery seeds
- 1/2 teaspoon onion powder
- 1/2 teaspoon garlic powder
- 1/2 teaspoon salt
- 1 pound chicken wings, cut up
- 1/2 tablespoon Worcestershire sauce
- Red pepper flakes, to taste

Directions

1. Brown chicken wings in a nonstick skillet until golden brown; transfer them to the slow cooker; set aside.
2. Mix the remaining ingredients in a pan over medium-high heat. Cook for a few minutes or until everything is well melted and incorporated.
3. Pour the sauce over the wings in the slow cooker; cook 7 hours 30 minutes on Low. Serve warm with your favorite dipping sauce.

– CHICKEN –

35. Peppery Chicken Curry

This is a great comfort food with a little spicy kick! If you don't have shallots, substitute with white or yellow onion.

Ready in about
4 hours
40 minutes

NUTRITIONAL INFORMATION
(Per Serving)

266 - Calories
10.2g - Fat
23.5g - Carbs
26.2g - Protein
3.3g - Sugars

Ingredients

- 1 garlic clove, finely minced
- 1/4 teaspoon freshly ground black pepper, to taste
- 1/2 cup red pepper flakes
- 1 tablespoon curry powder
- 1/4 teaspoon sea salt
- 1/2 tablespoon ginger, ground
- 1 cup chicken breasts, skinless and cubed
- 1/2 cup shallots, thinly sliced
- 1/2 cup chicken broth
- 1/4 cup non-dairy milk
- 1/2 Serrano pepper, seeded and chopped

Directions

1. Whisk together the broth, milk, garlic, curry powder, and ginger. Add the mixture to the slow cooker.
2. Lay the chicken on the sauce. Then, stir in the pepper and shallot. Season with salt, black pepper, and red pepper.
3. Cover and cook on High approximately 4 hours 30 minutes. Serve immediately.

– CHICKEN –

36. Ginger Chicken Thighs

Ginger is among the healthiest ingredients on the Earth. In addition to being super delicious, it is proven herbal medicine for thousands of years.

Ready in about
5 hours
30 minutes

NUTRITIONAL INFORMATION
(Per Serving)

213 - Calories
12.5g - Fat
4.2g - Carbs
21g - Protein
1.3g - Sugars

Ingredients

- 1 pound chicken thighs, boneless and skinless
- 1 tablespoon olive oil
- Salt and ground black pepper, to taste
- 1/4 teaspoon ginger, grated
- 1/2 teaspoon dried thyme
- 1/2 teaspoon ground allspice
- 1/2 teaspoon mustard seeds
- 1/2 cup onions, thinly sliced
- 1 clove garlic, finely minced

Directions

1. In a microwave safe dish, combine the onions, garlic, olive oil, ginger, and allspice. Microwave for 2 ½ minutes. Stir and microwave 2 ½ minutes more.
2. Throw the chicken into your slow cooker. Sprinkle with some thyme, mustard seeds, salt, and ground black pepper.
3. Stir in the prepared onion mixture. Cook on Low for 5 hours. Serve warm.

– CHICKEN –

37. Sticky Chicken Drumsticks

With fresh zingy lime juice, various spices and flavorful black chicken meat, this recipe is delicious and extremely comforting. A high-quality barbecue sauce is one of the best flavor-enhancing ingredients you can ever use!

Ready in about
5 hours
40 minutes

NUTRITIONAL
INFORMATION
(Per Serving)

128 - Calories
2.7g - Fat
12g - Carbs
13.2g - Protein
8g - Sugars

Ingredients

- 1 teaspoon garlic powder
- 1/2 teaspoon ground black pepper, to your liking
- 1/2 teaspoon shallot powder
- 1/2 teaspoon cumin
- 1 teaspoon salt
- 1 tablespoon fresh lime juice
- 1 tablespoon dark molasses
- 1/2 tablespoon soy sauce
- 1 tablespoon balsamic vinegar
- 1 tablespoon barbecue sauce
- 2 chicken drumsticks

Directions

1. Arrange the chicken drumsticks on the bottom of your slow cooker.
2. In a mixing dish, whisk together the molasses, soy sauce, lime juice, balsamic vinegar, and barbecue sauce.
3. Whisk in salt, ground black pepper, cumin, shallot powder, and garlic powder.
4. Pour the sauce over the chicken in the slow cooker. Cook for 5 hours 30 minutes using Low heat setting; serve warm and enjoy.

– CHICKEN –

38. Honey-Glazed Chicken Wings

This is an easy and quick way to cook satisfying chicken wings for you and your loved one. Fresh parsley and smoked spices provide a depth of BBQ flavor, while raw honey and minced garlic complete the meal with their extraordinary notes.

Ready in about
5 hours
15 minutes

NUTRITIONAL INFORMATION
(Per Serving)

455 - Calories
12.3g - Fat
70.9g - Carbs
20.7g - Protein
69.7g - Sugars

Ingredients

- 1 tablespoon olive oil
- 1/2 cup raw honey
- 1/4 teaspoon freshly ground black pepper
- 1/2 teaspoon sea salt
- 1/2 teaspoon smoked paprika
- 1/4 teaspoon smoked cayenne pepper
- 4 chicken wings
- 1/2 tablespoon fresh parsley, chopped
- 1 clove garlic, minced

Directions

1. Lay the chicken wings on the bottom of your slow cooker.
2. In a measuring cup, combine together the honey, garlic, olive oil, smoked paprika, cayenne pepper, salt, and ground black pepper.
3. Drizzle the honey mixture over the chicken wings. Cook for 5 hours on Low. Serve warm, topped with fresh parsley.

– CHICKEN –

39. Italian Sausage and Chicken in Tomato Sauce

A medley of spacy sausage, chicken meat and tomato sauce are flavored with amazing spices in this hearty and delicious meal for two people. Serve immediately over polenta.

Ready in about
5 hours
40 minutes

NUTRITIONAL INFORMATION
(Per Serving)

576 - Calories
37.9g - Fat
13.5g - Carbs
43.6g - Protein
8.6g - Sugars

Ingredients

- 1 chicken breast, boneless and skinless
- 1/2 tablespoon olive oil
- 1 tomato, diced
- 1 clove garlic, sliced
- 2 spicy Italian sausage links
- 1/2 cup vegetable broth
- 1/4 teaspoon dried rosemary
- 1/2 teaspoon dried basil
- 1/2 teaspoon salt
- 1/2 teaspoon dried oregano
- 1 tablespoon fresh sage, chopped
- 1/4 cup white vinegar
- 1/2 cup yellow onion, thinly sliced
- 10 ounces canned tomato sauce

Directions

1. Lay Italian sausage and chicken breasts on the bottom of your slow cooker.
2. Then, scatter the onions and garlic over it. Add the remaining ingredients and stir until everything is well combined.
3. Slow cook, covered, for 5 hours 30 minutes on Low. Serve warm.

– CHICKEN –

40. Greek-Style Chicken Stew

Mediterranean spices, chicken meat, and different types of vegetables. Sounds yummy! Alternatively, you can use some chili powder to add extra warmth to this amazing stew. Serve hot over cooked quinoa and enjoy!

Ready in about
5 hours
40 minutes

NUTRITIONAL INFORMATION
(Per Serving)

529 - Calories
16.1g - Fat
23.4g - Carbs
72.1g - Protein
10.4g Sugars

Ingredients

- 1 zucchini, sliced
- 1/2 onion, finely chopped
- 1 pound chicken, cubed
- 1 bay leaf
- 2 tablespoons Greek olives, pitted and chopped
- 1/2 carrot, thinly sliced
- 1/2 cup red bell pepper, thinly sliced
- 2 tomatoes, chopped
- 1/4 cup green bell pepper, thinly sliced
- 1/2 parsnip, chopped
- 2 cloves garlic, finely minced
- 1/4 teaspoon dried oregano
- 1/2 teaspoon red pepper flakes, crushed
- 1/4 teaspoon sea salt
- 1/2 teaspoon freshly cracked black pepper
- 1/4 teaspoon turmeric powder
- 1/4 teaspoon dried basil
- 1/2 teaspoon cumin seeds
- 1 tablespoon olive oil
- 1 cup chicken broth

Directions

1. In your slow cooker, warm olive oil over medium heat; sauté the onions and garlic until tender. Add the chicken cubes and brown them for 6 minutes longer.
2. Then, stir in the rest of the above ingredients; stir to combine well.
3. Now, cook your stew for 5 hours 30 minutes on Low heat. Serve and enjoy!

TURKEY

– TURKEY –

41. Turkey and Mushroom Chowder

Seasoned with thyme and bay leaf, this turkey dish has a unique flavor that brings a twist to your usual chowder. You can use a turkey leftover; if so, reduce the cooking time to 3 hours.

Ready in about
5 hours
15 minutes

NUTRITIONAL INFORMATION
(Per Serving)

320 - Calories
19.6g - Fat
11.4g - Carbs
24.4g - Protein
6.7g - Sugars

Ingredients

- 1 tablespoon butter
- 1/2 cup water
- 1 clove garlic, finely minced
- 1/2 cup heavy cream
- 2 ounces mushroom, sliced
- 1 cup chicken broth
- 1/2 teaspoon thyme
- 1/2 pound turkey breasts, diced
- 1 teaspoon seasoned salt, to taste
- 1 bay leaf
- 1/2 teaspoon black peppercorns
- 1/2 cup chicken broth
- 1 celery stalk, diced
- 1/2 cup onion, finely chopped

Directions

1. Simply place all ingredients in your slow cooker; stir to combine.
2. Next, slow cook the chowder for 5 hours on Low heat.
3. Serve warm and enjoy!

– TURKEY –

42. Hot Peppery Turkey Soup with Corn

Flavorful turkey soup with green chilies and canned tomatoes! This recipe has a delightful taste thanks to a dose of aromatic smoked paprika and chili powder. Enjoy!

Ready in about
6 hours
40 minutes

NUTRITIONAL INFORMATION
(Per Serving)

285 - Calories
2.4g - Fat
23g - Carbs
44g - Protein
10.3g - Sugars

Ingredients

- 1 cup cooked turkey breast, cut into bite-sized chunks
- 1 ounce canned diced green chilies, drained
- 1 Serrano peppers, diced
- 1/2 teaspoon smoked paprika
- 1 clove garlic, minced
- 8 ounces canned tomatoes, crushed
- 1/4 teaspoon salt
- 1/2 teaspoon chili powder
- 1/4 cup fresh corn kernels
- 2 cups turkey stock
- 1/2 medium shallot, diced

Directions

1. Place the canned tomatoes, turkey stock, shallot, garlic, chili powder, smoked paprika, and salt in your slow cooker.
2. Give it a good stir; put on the lid, and slow cook on Low setting for 5 hours.
3. After that, add the chilies, Serrano pepper, turkey and corn kernels. Cook, covered, for an additional 1 hour 30 minutes. Enjoy!

– TURKEY –

43. Hominy and Turkey Chili

For the very first time, make the recipe as written; later, you can experiment with seasonings according to your preferences. Serve this chili with your favorite fixings such as cooked rice, shredded yellow cheese, or homemade cornbread.

Ready in about 8 hours

NUTRITIONAL INFORMATION
(Per Serving)

187 - Calories
1.7g - Fat
28.1g - Carbs
15.7g - Protein
4.2g - Sugars

Ingredients

- 1/4 cooked turkey breast, cubed
- 1/3 cup cooked or canned cannellini beans, drained and rinsed
- 2 teaspoons lemon juice
- 1/4 teaspoon cumin
- 1 teaspoon celery seeds
- 1 teaspoon paprika
- 1/2 cup red onion, finely chopped
- 1/3 cup canned hominy, drained
- 1 chipotle in adobo sauce, minced

Directions

1. Put all ingredients, except the turkey, into your slow cooker.
2. Stir to mix well. Cook on Low setting for 7 hours.
3. Next, add the turkey and cook on High for an additional 40 minutes. Bon appétit!

– TURKEY –

44. Zucchini Noodles with Turkey and Vegetables

This richly flavored turkey dish is a perfect second-day dish after Thanksgiving. Comforting, warming and economical!

Ready in about 5 hours

NUTRITIONAL INFORMATION
(Per Serving)

387 - Calories
17.9g - Fat
20.7g - Carbs
37.3g - Protein
13.1g - Sugars

Ingredients

- 1 clove garlic, smashed
- 1/2 cup coconut milk
- 1/2 cup turkey stock
- 1 carrot, chopped
- Salt and ground black pepper, to taste
- 1 zucchini, julienned
- 1 pound skinless turkey breasts, diced
- 1/2 medium-sized onion, chopped
- 1/2 teaspoon red pepper flakes, crushed
- 1/4 cup chopped fresh cilantro, for garnish

Directions

1. Brown the turkey breasts in a pan over medium heat, stirring periodically.
2. In a lightly greased slow cooker, mix together the turkey stock, coconut milk, red pepper flakes, salt, and black pepper. Lay browned chicken breasts onto this mixture.
3. Then, lay the onions, garlic, carrots, and zucchini, on the turkey breasts. Cook for 4 hours 30 minutes on Low heat setting.
4. To serve, ladle the turkey mixture into individual serving bowls. Sprinkle with fresh cilantro and enjoy!

– TURKEY –

45. Turkey Chili with Cheddar Cheese

This chili has a deep flavor thanks to the smoky-sweet chilies in adobo. If you prefer a really hot dish, drizzle each serving with the chili oil.

Ready in about
9 hours
40 minutes

NUTRITIONAL INFORMATION
(Per Serving)

330 - Calories
13.7g - Fat
28.5g - Carbs
27.1g - Protein
6.6g - Sugars

Ingredients

- 10 ounces canned chili beans, drained and rinsed
- 1 leek, thinly sliced
- 2 bay leaves
- 1/2 teaspoon hot paprika
- 1 clove garlic, crushed
- 1 cup ground turkey
- 1/2 teaspoon black peppercorns
- 1/4 cup Cheddar cheese, shredded
- 10 ounces canned fire-roasted tomatoes, diced
- 1/2 teaspoon liquid smoke
- 1 chipotle chilies in adobo, finely minced

Directions

1. Quickly sear the meat in a pan until just warmed through. Drain off any excess fat. Transfer the seared turkey to the slow cooker.
2. Now, throw in chili beans, chilies in adobo, and canned fire-roasted tomatoes. Stir to combine well.
3. Next, add liquid smoke, paprika, leeks, garlic, bay leaf, and black peppercorns. Give it a good stir, and put on the lid. Cook on Low for 9 hours 30 minutes.
4. After that, open the lid and divide the chili among individual serving bowls. Lastly, top with shredded Cheddar cheese and serve hot. Enjoy!

– TURKEY –

46. Turkey, Mushroom and Ham Chowder

Serve this creamy chowder as an impressive first course or whenever you are craving a warm, hearty dish. Don't throw away the turkey carcass after holidays. Make amazing turkey stock and freeze leftovers for another meal!

Ready in about
5 hours
40 minutes

NUTRITIONAL INFORMATION
(Per Serving)

327 - Calories
17.7g - Fat
14.2g - Carbs
28.7g - Protein
3.9g - Sugars

Ingredients

- 2 ounces mushroom, thinly sliced
- 1/4 pound ham, cooked and diced
- 1 clove garlic, minced
- 1/4 cup heavy cream
- 1/2 parsnip, diced
- 1/2 onion, finely chopped
- 1/2 teaspoon thyme
- 1/2 celery stalk, diced
- 1/2 teaspoon salt
- 1 cup turkey stock
- 1/2 teaspoon granulated garlic
- 1 tablespoon butter
- 1 cup turkey breasts, diced
- 1/2 teaspoon cayenne pepper
- 1 cup water

Directions

1. Preheat the slow cooker and warm the butter over medium heat. Then, sauté the onion and garlic until they are just soft.
2. Once the time is up, stir in the remaining items; cook for 5 hours 30 minutes on Low setting.
3. Divide the soup among individual bowls and serve warm.

– TURKEY –

47. New Potatoes, Turkey and Kale Stew

If you're looking for a rich and healthy stew, a slow cooker is here to help! If you don't have new potatoes on hand, feel free to use sweet potatoes.

Ready in about
4 hours
15 minutes

NUTRITIONAL INFORMATION
(Per Serving)

203 - Calories
1.2g - Fat
36.7g - Carbs
13.6g - Protein
8.5g - Sugars

Ingredients

- 1 new potato, peeled and cubed
- 1/2 cup turkey stock
- 1 garlic clove, minced
- Sea salt and black pepper, to taste
- 1/2 parsnip, chopped
- 1/2 cup tomato puree
- 1/4 red pepper flakes, crushed
- 1/2 teaspoon capers
- 1 carrot, chopped
- 1/2 cup shallots, diced
- 1 cup skinless boneless turkey breast, cut into bite-size chunks
- 1 cup kale, torn into pieces

Directions

1. Grease the slow cooker with a little oil. Place the turkey on the bottom of your slow cooker. Top with shallots.
2. Lay new potatoes, carrots, and parsnip on the top of the shallots. The, add minced garlic, stock, tomato puree, and capers. Slow cook for 3 hours 30 minutes on Low setting.
3. Once the time is up, add the salt, black pepper, red pepper flakes, and kale. Continue to cook for 30 minutes more. Bon appétit!

– TURKEY –

48. Turkey Cocktail Meatballs

You can't go wrong with meatballs, right? You can serve these aromatic cheesy balls with tortillas and turn them into the main course.

Ready in about
6 hours
30 minutes

NUTRITIONAL INFORMATION
(Per Serving)

547 - Calories
27.4g - Fat
13.4g - Carbs
60.3g - Protein
4.7g - Sugars

Ingredients

- 3/4 pound lean turkey meat, ground
- 1/4 cup of rolled oats
- 1 tablespoon fresh parsley, finely chopped
- 1/4 teaspoon ground black pepper
- 1/2 teaspoon shallot powder
- 1/2 teaspoon dried basil
- 1/2 teaspoon dried rosemary
- 3 ounces Fontina cheese, cut into 24 cubes
- 1 egg
- 10 ounces tomato, crushed
- 1/2 tablespoon olive oil
- Salt and cayenne pepper, to taste
- 1/4 teaspoon garlic powder
- 1/4 teaspoon dried oregano

Directions

1. To make the sauce, mix the tomato with olive oil. Then add the shallot powder, garlic powder, oregano, rosemary, parsley, and basil; mix to combine well using a spoon.
2. In another mixing bowl, combine the oats, ground turkey, eggs, salt, cayenne pepper, and ground black pepper. Then, shape the mixture into 8 balls.
3. Now, stuff each meatball with a cube of Fontina cheese.
4. Pour 1/2 of the tomato sauce in the slow cooker. Lay the meatballs on it; top with the rest of the sauce.
5. Cover the slow cooker; now, slow cook your meatballs for 6 hours on Low setting. Transfer them to a serving platter and enjoy your party!

– TURKEY –

49. Rich Cheese and Meat Dip

Here's the perfect idea for your next snack or brunch! Serve with veggie sticks, steamed broccoli florets or tortilla chips.

Ready in about
3 hours
40 minutes

NUTRITIONAL INFORMATION
(Per Serving)

341 - Calories
19.1g - Fat
16.8g - Carbs
27.8g - Protein
4.9g - Sugars

Ingredients

- 1 cup ground turkey
- 1 small-sized can tomatoes with chilies
- 1/2 pound Ricotta cheese
- 1/2 cup sausage, sliced
- 1/2 teaspoon garlic powder
- 1/2 teaspoon onion powder
- 1/2 bell pepper, seeded and chopped
- 1/2 can cream of celery soup

Directions

1. Mix the cheese, tomatoes with chilies, cream of celery soup, onion powder, garlic powder, and chopped bell pepper in your slow cooker; heat until everything is melted and incorporated.
2. Meanwhile, brown ground turkey and sliced sausage in a sauté pan over medium flame. Crumble the meat and drain excess grease. Add the meat mixture to the slow cooker.
3. Give it a good stir. Cook for 3 hours 30 minutes on Low. Serve warm. Lovely!

– TURKEY –

50. Thanksgiving Turkey with Fruit

Good turkey breasts deserve the best fruit! This fun recipe that combines unusual flavors will improve your holiday table. Enjoy!

Ready in about
7 hours
40 minutes

NUTRITIONAL INFORMATION
(Per Serving)

341 - Calories
19.1g - Fat
16.8g - Carbs
27.8g - Protein
4.9g - Sugars

Ingredients

- 2 tablespoons raw honey
- 1 cup pears, cored and sliced
- 1/2 cup apples, cored and sliced
- 1/4 teaspoon allspice
- 1/2 teaspoon white pepper, to taste
- 1/4 teaspoon salt
- 1/2 turkey breast
- 2 tablespoons balsamic vinegar
- 1/4 cup golden raisins

Directions

1. Arrange turkey breast on the bottom of your slow cooker. Arrange the pears, apples, and golden raisins around the turkey breasts.
2. Season with salt, allspice, and white pepper.
3. Drizzle balsamic vinegar and honey over all. Set the slow cooker to Low heat; place the lid on it.
4. Cook on Low for 7 hours 30 minutes or until everything is cooked through. Bon appétit!

– TURKEY –

51. Lime Turkey Breasts

Cooked the traditional way, turkey breasts can become dull and tasteless. Slow cooking improves textures and extracts a meaty flavor in your dish!

Ready in about
4 hours
40 minutes

NUTRITIONAL INFORMATION
(Per Serving)

231 - Calories
3.4g - Fat
17.5g - Carbs
31.7g - Protein
11.9g - Sugars

Ingredients

- 1 carrot, cut into coins
- 1/2 cup chicken broth
- 1/2 onion, chopped
- 1/2 turkey breasts
- 1 tablespoon fresh lime juice
- 1 garlic clove, minced
- 1/4 teaspoon cayenne pepper, to your liking
- 1/4 teaspoon paprika
- Sea salt and black pepper, to your liking
- 1 bell pepper, seeded and diced

Directions

1. Lay the turkey breasts on the bottom of your slow cooker. Season with salt, black pepper, cayenne pepper, and paprika.
2. Add the remaining ingredients. Turn the slow cooker to High heat.
3. Cook for 4 hours 30 minutes or until the chicken is thoroughly cooked. Serve immediately and enjoy!

– TURKEY –

52. Hash Browns with Turkey Bacon

Red skin potatoes go perfectly with browned turkey bacon in this simple and delicious meal for two. You can add fresh minced garlic or garlic powder if desired. Serve with sweet corn.

Ready in about
4 hours
40 minutes

NUTRITIONAL INFORMATION
(Per Serving)

227 - Calories
3.2g - Fat
34.3g - Carbs
13.6g - Protein
3.6g Sugars

Ingredients

- 3/4 pound red skin potatoes, thinly sliced
- 1/2 tablespoon Dijon mustard
- 1/2 cup onion, sliced into thin rings
- 1 strip turkey bacon, diced
- 1/2 teaspoon olive oil
- Salt and ground black pepper, to your liking

Directions

1. Heat olive oil in a cast-iron skillet. Add bacon and sauté until just browned.
2. Add sautéed bacon the slow cooker. Stir in the remaining ingredients.
3. Cook on Low for 4 hours 30 minutes.
   Bon appétit!

– TURKEY –

53. Turkey and Habanero Dip

Say "Cheese" and indulge in this fantastic dipping sauce! This is the perfect winter snack to cheer you up immediately. Serve with herb croutons.

Ready in about
1 hour
40 minutes

NUTRITIONAL INFORMATION
(Per Serving)

440 - Calories
29.1g - Fat
13.3g - Carbs
35.3g - Protein
4.3g - Sugars

Ingredients

- 1/2 Habanero pepper, seeded and finely chopped
- 1/2 bell pepper, chopped
- 2 ounces Colby cheese, shredded
- 2 ounces cream cheese
- 1 cup ground turkey
- 1/2 teaspoon dried thyme
- Salt and ground black pepper, to taste
- 1/2 teaspoon garlic powder
- 1 small-sized shallot, chopped
- 1 can refried beans
- 4 ounces picante sauce

Directions

1. First, cook the shallot and ground turkey until the shallot is translucent; discard any excess fat. Transfer the turkey/shallot mixture to the slow cooker.
2. Add the remaining ingredients.
3. Cook, stirring occasionally, for 1 hour 30 minutes on Low setting.

– TURKEY –

54. Delicious Velveeta and Turkey Dip

This magical recipe calls for Velveeta, flavorsome cheese with great meltability. You really deserve this meaty goodness!

Ready in about
1 hours
40 minutes

NUTRITIONAL INFORMATION
(Per Serving)

423 - Calories
26.2g - Fat
16.9g - Carbs
36.4g - Protein
8.2g - Sugars

Ingredients

- 1 cup Velveeta cheese, diced
- 1/2 can tomatoes
- 1/2 cup picante sauce
- 1 cup ground turkey
- 1/2 teaspoon mustard seeds
- 1/2 teaspoon garlic powder
- 1/2 cup turkey sausage
- 1/4 teaspoon dried oregano
- 1/2 teaspoon onion powder
- 2 sprigs dried rosemary, crushed
- 1/2 teaspoon cumin
- 1/4 teaspoon dried basil
- 1/2 can cream of celery soup

Directions

1. First of all, brown ground turkey and sausage for a few minutes; crumble and drain the excess fat. Transfer the browned meat to the slow cooker.
2. Combine the remaining ingredients in a mixing dish; whisk to combine well. Now, add the mixture to the slow cooker.
3. Cook on Low setting until cheese is completely melted and everything is thoroughly cooked or 1 hour 30 minutes. Serve with your favorite dippers.

– TURKEY –

55. Turkey with Chickpeas and Veggies

You probably stumbled across this turkey meal at some point. Now, you can serve it warm from your slow cooker. Lovely!

Ready in about
5 hours
40 minutes

NUTRITIONAL
INFORMATION
(Per Serving)

487 - Calories
8.7g - Fat
66.6g - Carbs
38.2g - Protein
17.5g - Sugars

Ingredients

- 5 ounces chickpeas
- 1/2 red onion, chopped
- 1/2 carrot, sliced
- 1 cup grape tomatoes
- 1/4 teaspoon granulated garlic
- 1/4 teaspoon onion powder
- 1/2 teaspoon turmeric
- Black pepper and salt, to your liking
- 1/2 teaspoon cumin
- 1/2 celery, chopped
- 1/2 cup zucchini, sliced
- 1 cup turkey, boneless and cubed
- 1/2 cup chicken broth
- 1/2 red bell pepper, sliced
- 1/2 parsnip, chopped
- 1/2 green bell pepper, sliced

Directions

1. Place all of the ingredients in your slow cooker; cook the mixture for 5 hours 30 minutes on Low setting.
2. Serve immediately.

PORK

– PORK –

56. Saucy Pork Chops with Apricots

Pair pork and apricots with canned tomatoes in this easy and sophisticated dish. Serve with homemade crusty bread!

Ready in about
5 hours
40 minutes

NUTRITIONAL INFORMATION
(Per Serving)

431 - Calories
27.6g - Fat
24.8g - Carbs
20.8g - Protein
5.2g - Sugars

Ingredients

- 1 cup canned tomatoes with their juice
- 1 tablespoon olive oil
- 1/4 teaspoon ginger, ground
- 1/2 cup beef broth
- 2 pork loin chops
- 1/2 teaspoon cayenne pepper
- 1 onion, chopped
- 2 tablespoons fresh cilantro, chopped
- Salt and freshly ground black pepper, to your liking
- 1/4 cup water
- 1/4 cup dried apricots, coarsely chopped
- 1 tablespoon cornstarch mixed with 2 tablespoons of water

Directions

1. Season the pork loin chops with salt, black pepper, and cayenne pepper. In a large-sized skillet, heat the olive oil over medium-high heat.
2. Then, sear the pork in hot oil. Transfer the pork to the slow cooker.
3. In the same skillet, in the meat drippings and juices, over medium heat, sauté the onions and ginger until the onions begin to soften slightly.
4. Pour a small amount of the water or broth into the pan to scrape up any browned bits. Transfer the contents of the skillet to the slow cooker.
5. Next, add the beef broth, water, apricots, and tomatoes. Seal the cooker, and cook on High for 5 hours 30 minutes. Transfer the pork chops to a serving platter.
6. Bring the sauce to a boil, and stir in the cornstarch mixture. Now, whisk until the sauce is thickened. Serve the pork chops garnished with the sauce, and topped with fresh cilantro. Enjoy!

57. Soft Pork Tenderloin with Apples

Pork tenderloin and apples make an excellent Sunday lunch for you and your beloved one. You can add some extra spices such as mustard powder, ground bay leaves or cumin.

Ready in about
7 hours
40 minutes

NUTRITIONAL INFORMATION
(Per Serving)

257 - Calories
4.4g - Fat
25g - Carbs
30.2g - Protein
20.3g - Sugars

Ingredients

- 1 apple, cored and sliced
- 1 tablespoon raw honey
- 1/2 teaspoon dried basil
- 1 teaspoon cayenne pepper
- 1/2 teaspoon dried oregano
- Salt and ground black pepper, to your liking
- 1/2 teaspoon dried dill weed
- 1/2 pound pork tenderloin

Directions

1. Place the pork tenderloin in the slow cooker.
2. Arrange the apples around the pork. Season with dill weed, basil, oregano, salt, black pepper, and cayenne pepper.
3. Drizzle raw honey over everything and cook for 7 hours 30 minutes on Low. Serve warm.

– PORK –

58. Pork with Spinach, Apple and Pear

Flavorful fruits and spinach balance pork meat in this tasty and unusual dish! This is a true comfort food for any occasion.

Ready in about
7 hours
10 minutes

NUTRITIONAL
INFORMATION
(Per Serving)

453 - Calories
24.8g - Fat
23.9g - Carbs
34g - Protein
18.9g - Sugars

Ingredients

- 1 cup spinach leaves, torn into pieces
- 1 tablespoon lemon juice
- 1/2 cup apple, cored and quartered
- 1/2 pound pork loin, excess fat removed
- 1/2 cup pear, cored and quartered
- 1/4 teaspoon cayenne pepper
- 1/4 teaspoon ground black pepper
- 1/4 teaspoon dried dill weed
- 1/2 teaspoon salt
- 1 tablespoon honey
- 1/2 tablespoon nut butter
- Pomegranate seeds, for garnish

Directions

1. Lay the pork loin on the bottom of a lightly oiled slow cooker. Then, spread honey over the pork; then, arrange the apples and pears around the pork.
2. Add nut butter; slow cook on Low for 6 hours 30 minutes.
3. Then, stir in the spinach and cook an additional 40 minutes. Drizzle with lemon juice.
4. Season with dill, salt, black pepper, and cayenne pepper. Adjust the seasonings, and serve sprinkled with pomegranate seeds.

– PORK –

59. Cheese and Bacon Dip

If you're looking for a traditional dip recipe with a little bit of oomph, this bacon and cheese mixture might be right for you! Worcestershire sauce adds a deep flavor to the whole thing.

Ready in about
1 hour
30 minutes

NUTRITIONAL INFORMATION
(Per Serving)

455 - Calories
33.4g - Fat
6.6g - Carbs
30.9g - Protein
1g - Sugars

Ingredients

- 4 ounces Cottage cheese, softened and cubed
- 1 teaspoon Worcestershire sauce
- 1/2 cup half-and-half
- 1/2 cup Cheddar cheese, shredded
- 1/2 teaspoon ground black pepper
- 1/4 teaspoon dry mustard
- 1/4 teaspoon salt
- 4 slices bacon, diced, fried and drained
- 1/2 small-sized onion, finely chopped

Directions

1. Put all ingredients into the slow cooker.
2. Cook on Low setting, stirring occasionally, until the cheese has melted, about 1 hour 15 minutes.
3. Taste and adjust the seasonings. Serve with cubed toasted bread.

– PORK –

60. Pork and Bacon with Mango Sauce

This pork recipe will change your perception of meat dishes. Tender, juicy, and fruity, it is sure to please!

Ready in about
7 hours
40 minutes

NUTRITIONAL
INFORMATION
(Per Serving)

485 - Calories
7.5g - Fat
38.2g - Carbs
37.5g - Protein
25.3g - Sugars

Ingredients

- 1/2 pound pork loin, silver skin and excess fat removed
- 1 ripe mango, pitted and diced
- 2 tablespoons apple cider vinegar
- 3 tablespoons water
- 1/2 tablespoon brown sugar
- 1/2 teaspoon salt
- 1/2 teaspoon smoked cayenne pepper
- 1/2 teaspoon freshly cracked black pepper
- 1 tablespoon fresh ginger, peeled and minced
- 1 small-sized shallot, chopped
- 1 tablespoon lower-sodium soy sauce
- 1 slice bacon

Directions

1. In a cast-iron skillet, fry the bacon over medium heat; fry for 6 minutes; then, crumble it; transfer it to the slow cooker along with the drippings.
2. Dump the remaining ingredients into the slow cooker.
3. Slow cook for 7 hours 30 minutes and don't lift the lid too much. Adjust the seasonings. Divide the pork among serving plates; ladle the mango sauce over it and serve immediately.

– PORK –

61. Smoky Spare Ribs

Looking for a simple and effective recipe for spare ribs? You can have restaurant-style ribs at your own home! Serve over hot rice.

Ready in about
9 hours
15 minutes

NUTRITIONAL
INFORMATION
(Per Serving)

252 - Calories
5.5g - Fat
7.8g - Carbs
42.1g - Protein
3.2g - Sugars

Ingredients

- 1 tablespoon white wine vinegar
- Sea salt and black pepper, to taste
- 1/4 teaspoon ground cinnamon
- 1/2 teaspoon smoked cayenne pepper
- 1/2 cup water
- 5 ounces canned tomatoes, crushed
- 1/4 teaspoon liquid smoke
- 1 pound pork spare ribs
- 1 dried chipotle pepper, chopped
- 1/2 shallot, chopped
- 1 tablespoon soy sauce
- 1 clove garlic, minced

Directions

1. Rub the pork ribs with smoked cayenne pepper, sea salt, and black pepper. Lay the rubbed pork ribs on the bottom of your slow cooker.
2. Then, add the remaining ingredients in the order listed above.
3. Cook on Low setting for 9 hours and serve warm.

– PORK –

62. Hash Brown Breakfast Casserole with Bacon

The old-fashioned hash brown casserole is as delicious as it looks. Slow cooking is one of the best cooking methods to make the hash browns. Give it a try!

Ready in about
9 hours
20 minutes

NUTRITIONAL INFORMATION
(Per Serving)

409 - Calories
24.9g - Fat
27.4g - Carbs
19.5g - Protein
4.6g - Sugars

Ingredients

- 1/4 cup Colby cheese, grated
- 1 clove garlic, finely minced
- 2 scallions, finely chopped
- 1/2 bell pepper, diced
- 1/2 cup cooked bacon, crumbled
- 4 ounces hash browns, frozen
- 2 eggs, slightly beaten
- 1/2 teaspoon dried rosemary, crushed
- 1/2 teaspoon freshly cracked black pepper
- 1 teaspoon smoked paprika
- 1/4 teaspoon salt
- 1/2 teaspoon dried basil
- 1/4 cup milk

Directions

1. Arrange a layer of hash browns on the bottom of the slow cooker. Now, add a layer of bacon, then scallion, bell peppers, grated cheese, and garlic.
2. Repeat the layering process, ending with a layer of grated cheese.
3. In a mixing dish, combine the remaining ingredients; beat until everything is well combined. Pour the mixture over the mixture in your slow cooker.
4. Cover and slow cook for 9 hours on Low. Eat warm and enjoy!

– PORK –

63. Pork Tenderloin with Vermouth Sauce

There are many reasons you should be cooking with lard. For example, it has less saturated fat than butter! Some of the best restaurants in the world choose the lard to make their pies, biscuits and vegetable dishes.

Ready in about
4 hours
40 minutes

NUTRITIONAL
INFORMATION
(Per Serving)

226 - Calories
7.3g - Fat
5.1g - Carbs
30.5g - Protein
2.3g - Sugars

Ingredients

- 1/2 pound pork tenderloin
- 1/2 tablespoon Vermouth
- 1 garlic clove, chopped
- 1 jalapeño pepper, seeded and minced
- 1/2 onion, chopped
- 1/2 tablespoon lard, room temperature
- 1 teaspoon sea salt
- 1/2 teaspoon smoked cayenne pepper
- 1/2 teaspoon ground cumin
- 1/2 cup roasted-vegetable broth
- 1 tomato, diced

Directions

1. Brush the sides and bottom of your slow cooker with the lard. Lay the pork tenderloin on the bottom of the slow cooker
2. Then, arrange the remaining ingredients around the pork. Now cook for 4 hours 30 minutes on Low setting.
3. Serve the pork with cooking liquid on the side. Enjoy!

– PORK –

64. Saucy Pork Ribs

Slow cooking is one of the cooking methods that best retains nutrients in your food. Try making your own 5-spice powder by simply mixing the equal amount of cinnamon, cloves, Szechuan peppercorns, toasted fennel seeds, and star anise.

Ready in about
5 hours
30 minutes

NUTRITIONAL INFORMATION
(Per Serving)

345 - Calories
20.5g - Fat
3.7g - Carbs
31.6g - Protein
2.1g - Sugars

Ingredients

- 1/2 cup vegetable broth
- 1 tablespoon Worcestershire sauce
- 1 clove garlic, minced
- 1/2 cup water
- 1/2 pound pork ribs
- 1/2 teaspoon sea salt
- 1/2 teaspoon ground black pepper
- 1/2 teaspoon Chinese 5-spice powder
- 1 scallion, chopped
- 1/2 cup white vinegar

Directions

1. Place the pork ribs on the bottom of the slow cooker; top with scallions and garlic. Now, drizzle the water, vinegar, and vegetable broth over all.
2. Season with sea salt and ground black pepper; then, allow the mixture to stand overnight.
3. Add Worcestershire sauce and Chinese 5-spice powder.
4. Cook on High heat for 5 hours. Serve immediately!

– PORK –

65. Sautéed Pork Sausage with Sauerkraut

Just like grandma used to make pork sausages! Slowly, healthy, with love...
Serve with your favorite salad and enough crusty bread.

Ready in about
4 hours
40 minutes

NUTRITIONAL INFORMATION
(Per Serving)

449 - Calories
30.7g - Fat
20.8g - Carbs
22.7g - Protein
14.8g Sugars

Ingredients

- 1/2 tablespoon bacon fat
- 1 cup unsweetened applesauce
- 1 cup sauerkraut, rinsed and drained
- 1 teaspoon fennel seeds
- 1/2 red onion, sliced
- 1 bay leaf
- 2 small-sized pork sausages
- 1/2 teaspoon black peppercorns
- 1 clove garlic, minced

Directions

1. Dump all of the above ingredients into your slow cooker.
2. Cook about 4 hours 30 minutes on Low setting. Serve immediately. Bon appétit!

– PORK –

66. Super Yummy Pork Sausage Pie

Pork sausage is affordable and tasty dinner idea. Fresh, healthy yam and succulent sausage work together to create a splendidly tasty pie.

Ready in about
7 hours
30 minutes

**NUTRITIONAL INFORMATION
(Per Serving)**

476 - Calories
37.2g - Fat
16.9g - Carbs
27.3g - Protein
3.6g - Sugars

Ingredients

- 2 small-sized pork sausages
- 1/2 bell pepper, chopped
- 2 eggs, whisked
- 1/2 onion, peeled and finely chopped
- 1/2 teaspoon dried rosemary
- 1/2 teaspoon garlic powder
- 1/2 teaspoon dried basil
- 1 teaspoon dried oregano
- 1/2 teaspoon fennel seeds
- 1/2 yam, shredded
- Kosher salt and ground black pepper, to taste
- Nonstick cooking spray

Directions

1. Treat your slow cooker with a nonstick cooking spray.
2. Then, add all ingredients to the slow cooker; mix well to combine.
3. Place on Low heat for 7 hours or until thoroughly cooked.
4. Let it cool slightly before slicing and serving. Slice into wedges and enjoy!

– PORK –

67. Ham and Bean Soup with Kale

Here is a cheap and easy lunch idea that is sure to please. Winter days call for something warm and piquant; spice them up and add a few sprinkles of chili pepper and mustard seeds.

Ready in about
8 hours
10 minutes

NUTRITIONAL INFORMATION
(Per Serving)

328 - Calories
8.5g - Fat
61.1g - Carbs
27.5g - Protein
8g - Sugars

Ingredients

- 1/2 tablespoon canola oil
- 1/2 teaspoon hot sauce
- 1 green garlic, minced
- 1 carrot, finely chopped
- 1/4 pound ham, finely chopped
- 5 ounces canned chicken stock
- 1/4 cup Vidalia, finely chopped
- 1/2 teaspoon Cajun seasoning
- 1 cup dried navy beans
- 2 bay leaves
- 1/2 cup kale, washed and torn into pieces

Directions

1. Place beans in a large-sized saucepan over medium-high heat. Bring to a boil, stirring frequently. After that, turn off burner. Allow beans to soften about 50 minutes.
2. Then, drain beans in a colander; rinse beans and transfer them to the slow cooker.
3. Meanwhile, heat canola oil in a nonstick skillet over medium heat. Now, add the ham, Vidalia, green garlic, carrots, and kale. Sauté, stirring continuously, until your veggies are tender, 5 to 6 minutes. Transfer vegetables to the slow cooker.
4. Stir in the remaining ingredients. Add water so your slow cooker is three-quarters full.
5. Lastly, cover the cooker and cook on Low setting for about 7 hours. Serve hot.

– PORK –

68. French-Style Lentil Soup

Lentils are easy to cook and they are actually one of the tastiest staples in every diet. This lentil soup is so tasty, you won't even believe it's healthy. This soup reheats well too.

Ready in about
8 hours
40 minutes

NUTRITIONAL
INFORMATION
(Per Serving)

439 - Calories
2.3g - Fat
76.9g - Carbs
28g - Protein
9.4g - Sugars

Ingredients

- 2 cups water
- 1/2 teaspoon garlic paste
- 1 tomato, diced
- 1 cup green lentils, rinsed
- 1/2 cup sweet onions, chopped
- 2 tablespoons fresh cilantro, minced
- 1/4 cup parsnip, chopped
- A pinch of ground black pepper
- 1/2 tablespoon sugar
- 1/4 teaspoon dried oregano
- 1/2 teaspoon dried basil
- 1/4 teaspoon salt
- 1/2 cup carrots, chopped
- 1/2 ham bone
- 1 tablespoon white wine vinegar
- 1/4 cup celery, chopped
- 1/2 cup croutons, for serving

Directions

1. Add ham bone, lentils, parsnip, celery, carrots, and sweet onions to your slow cooker.
2. Whisk garlic paste and cilantro with 1 cup of lukewarm water, and add it to the slow cooker. Pour in 2 cups of water.
3. Cover and slow cook on Low setting for 4 hours 30 minutes.
4. Then, combine tomato, sugar, basil, oregano, salt, black pepper, and white wine vinegar together in a mixing bowl.
5. Add it to the slow cooker, put on the lid and cook on Low setting for an additional 4 hours.
6. Remove the ham bone. Cut pieces of ham into bite-size chunks. Then, add the ham to the soup, and serve with croutons. Enjoy!

– PORK –

69. Easy Sausage and Velveeta Dip

Cooking spicy sausage in a slow cooker "locks" in the flavors. This is a delicious dipping sauce you'll be asked to cook time and time again.

Ready in about 50 minutes

NUTRITIONAL INFORMATION
(Per Serving)

476 - Calories
37.2g - Fat
9g - Carbs
26.9g - Protein
3.2g - Sugars

Ingredients

- 1 teaspoon canned chilies, minced
- 1/2 teaspoon salt
- 1/2 pound cooked spicy sausage, crumbled
- 1 teaspoon cayenne pepper
- 1/2 tablespoon fresh cilantro, roughly chopped
- 1/2 teaspoon ground black pepper
- 1/2 cup Velveeta cheese

Directions

1. Place all of the above ingredients in your slow cooker.
2. Cook on Low heat setting for 40 minute or until Velveeta is fully melted.
3. Serve warm with dippers such as tortilla chips or vegetable sticks. Enjoy!

– PORK –

70. Pork Strips with Pineapple

With slow cooked pork strips, making the most sophisticated festive dinner becomes a breeze! In this recipe, you can experiment with seasonings and adjust them to suit your taste.

Ready in about
9 hours
20 minutes

NUTRITIONAL INFORMATION
(Per Serving)

358 - Calories
11.3g - Fat
22.8g - Carbs
33g - Protein
17g - Sugars

Ingredients

- 3 ounces canned pineapple chunks
- 1/4 cup barbecue sauce
- 1 scallion, chopped
- 1 garlic clove, crushed
- 1 ½ tablespoons tamari sauce
- 2 tablespoons dry sherry
- 1/2 pound lean pork, cut into strips, browned
- 1/4 teaspoon kosher salt
- 1 tablespoon brown sugar
- 1/2 teaspoon ground black pepper

Directions

1. Combine all ingredients, except for the pork strips, in your slow cooker.
2. Now, stir in the pork strips; stir to coat well. Cook on Low, covered, for 9 hours.

BEEF

– BEEF –

71. Easy Sunday Beef Sandwiches

This is probably the only recipe for beef sandwiches you'll ever need. Because this combination of flavors will satisfy literally everyone. You can choose your favorite fixings.

Ready in about
7 hours
20 minutes

NUTRITIONAL INFORMATION
(Per Serving)

365 - Calories
11.4g - Fat
28.9g - Carbs
40.3g - Protein
4.9g - Sugars

Ingredients

- 1 teaspoon mustard, for garnish
- 1/2 teaspoon ground black pepper, to your liking
- 1 bay leaf
- 1/2 teaspoon sea salt
- 1 cup of your favourite spaghetti sauce
- 1/4 cup beef stock
- 1/2 pound roast meat
- 2 English muffins
- 1/2 teaspoon black peppercorns

Directions

1. Simply drop all of the ingredients, except the mustard and English muffins, in your slow cooker. Slow cook for 7 hours on Low.
2. Remove the bay leaves; add your favourite mustard and stir to combine. Then, ladle over English muffins and serve warm. Enjoy!

– BEEF –

72. Cheesy Corn and Beef

With several layers of flavor, this rich, mellowly dish goes perfectly with crunchy lettuce and fresh radishes.

Ready in about
5 hours
40 minutes

NUTRITIONAL INFORMATION
(Per Serving)

468 - Calories
24.9g - Fat
19.9g - Carbs
42.5g - Protein
5.5g - Sugars

Ingredients

- 2 ounces Monterey Jack cheese, shredded
- 2 ounces Ricotta cheese
- 1 small-sized tomato, diced
- 1 cup beef, minced
- Salt and ground black pepper, to your liking
- 4 ounces sweet corn
- 1/4 cup beef broth
- 1 scallion, finely chopped
- 2 ounces Greek yogurt
- 1 tablespoon canola oil

Directions

1. First of all, heat the oil over medium flame. Then, brown the beef about 10 minutes, stirring constantly.
2. Now, stir in the scallion, corn, tomatoes, and broth.
3. Seal the slow cooker; cook for 4 hours 30 minutes on Low. Now, stir in the remaining items and cook for 1 hour more.
4. Once the time is up, serve warm.

– BEEF –

73. Spiced Beef and Pork with Vegetables

What we love most about using a slow cooker to cook meat with vegetables is that we can leave the cooker unattended. Finished with amazingly fragrant seasonings, this is a knockout dish for any occasion!

Ready in about
6 hours
50 minutes

NUTRITIONAL INFORMATION
(Per Serving)

281 - Calories
15.3g - Fat
10.8g - Carbs
25.5g - Protein
6g - Sugars

Ingredients

- 1/2 cup minced pork
- 4 ounces canned tomato sauce
- 1 clove garlic, finely chopped
- 1/2 cup minced beef
- 1/2 yellow onion, diced
- 1 tablespoon olive oil
- 1/2 teaspoon salt
- 1/2 teaspoon basil powder
- 1/2 crushed red pepper flakes, to taste
- 1/2 red bell pepper, seeded and diced
- 1/2 green bell pepper, seeded and diced
- 1/2 carrot, finely chopped
- 1 stalk celery, finely chopped
- 1/2 tablespoon cumin powder
- 1 green chili, finely minced

Directions

1. Heat your slow cooker and warm the oil over medium flame. Sauté the garlic and onion in hot olive oil for 5 minutes, stirring frequently.
2. Now, stir in the minced beef and pork; add green chilies, bell peppers, carrots, and celery. Sauté for 4 to 5 minutes longer.
3. Stir in the remaining items. Now, cook for 6 hours 30 minutes on Low and serve warm.

– BEEF –

74. Chipotle Beef and Pork Chili

It doesn't take a lot of effort to turn an ordinary chili into an outstanding, crave-worthy light meal. Be inspired!

Ready in about
9 hours
20 minutes

NUTRITIONAL INFORMATION
(Per Serving)

470 - Calories
24.8g - Fat
14.5g - Carbs
47.5g - Protein
5g - Sugars

Ingredients

- 8 ounces canned beans, drained and rinsed
- 6 ounces canned tomatoes diced
- 1 clove garlic, minced
- 1 chipotle in adobo, chopped
- 1/2 teaspoon chili powder
- 1/2 teaspoon smoked paprika
- 1/2 cup ground beef
- 1 cup ground pork
- 1/4 cup red onions, diced

Directions

1. In a nonstick skillet, sauté the beef and pork until they're thoroughly warmed. Drain off any excess fat. Transfer browned meat to the slow cooker.
2. Next, stir in the remaining ingredients. Stir to combine. Cook on Low for 9 hours.
3. Serve your chili in individual bowls. Bon appétit!

– BEEF –

75. Beer-Braised Chuck Roast

Looking for an amazing, traditional roast? This recipe may become your favorite holiday choice.

Cook's note: Opt for beers like Porter that will give caramelized and robust nutty flavors to your slow-cooked roast.

Ready in about
6 hours
40 minutes

NUTRITIONAL
INFORMATION
(Per Serving)

333 - Calories
12.2g - Fat
17.3g - Carbs
32.9g - Protein
1.2g - Sugars

Ingredients

- 1/2 cup beer
- 1 tablespoon butter
- 1/2 onion, sliced
- 2 tablespoons all-purpose flour
- 1/2 pound boneless chuck, cut into bite-sized cubes
- 1 clove garlic, minced
- 1 tablespoon all-purpose flour
- 1/2 teaspoon freshly cracked black pepper
- 1/2 teaspoon sea salt, to taste

Directions

1. Coat beef cubes with 2 tablespoons of flour. Then, melt the butter over medium heat. Fry the beef in the melted butter.
2. Transfer browned meat to the slow cooker; now, stir in the rest of the above ingredients.
3. Cover with the lid, and cook on Low for 6 hours. Turn the heat to High setting.
4. Dissolve remaining 1 tablespoon of flour in small amount of water. Pour into the meat mixture and slow cook about 30 minutes more. Serve over hot rice.

76. BBQ Pork and Beef Stew

(In this recipe, you can experiment with seasonings and adjust them to suit your taste. Ground bay leaf, cumin powder, a pinch of ground allspice work well too.

Ready in about
9 hours
20 minutes

NUTRITIONAL INFORMATION
(Per Serving)

450 - Calories
22.7g - Fat
21.2g - Carbs
38.5g - Protein
10.6g - Sugars

Ingredients

- 1 cup beef broth
- 1/2 pound stew meat
- 1/4 cup barbecue sauce
- 1/4 teaspoon ground black pepper
- 1 teaspoon sea salt
- 1/2 teaspoon cayenne pepper
- 3 ounces canned tomatoes
- 1 clove garlic, finely minced
- 1/2 small Habanero pepper, finely chopped
- 1/2 cup leeks, thinly sliced
- 1 tablespoon coconut oil
- 1 tablespoon cornstarch
- 2 tablespoons cold water

Directions

1. First, melt the coconut oil over medium heat. Cook the meat, leeks, and garlic in hot oil.
2. Add the remaining ingredients, except the cornstarch and water.
3. Cook on Low heat for 9 hours.
4. In a mixing dish, whisk the cornstarch in cold water; then, thicken your stew just before serving. Serve over boiled potatoes, if desired.

– Beef –

77. Saucy Cocktail Meatballs

These meatballs use only the most basic pantry staples and take 5 minutes to prepare. They are juicy and full of flavor. Serve with cocktail picks.

Ready in about 5 hours

NUTRITIONAL INFORMATION
(Per Serving)

441 - Calories
21.2g - Fat
23.5g - Carbs
39.9g - Protein
17.5g - Sugars

Ingredients

- 1/4 pound lean ground beef
- 1 tablespoon soy sauce
- 1 small-sized egg, slightly beaten
- 1/4 pound lean ground pork
- 1/2 seasoned salt
- 1/4 teaspoon black pepper
- 1 tablespoon packed brown sugar
- 1/4 teaspoon cayenne pepper
- 2 ounces canned tomato paste
- 2 tablespoons apple cider vinegar
- 1 tablespoon dry bread crumbs, seasoned
- 1/3 cup tomato ketchup

Directions

1. Preheat an oven to 350 degrees F. In a medium mixing bowl, combine ground pork, beef, 1 tablespoon ketchup, bread crumbs, egg, black pepper, cayenne pepper, and salt.
2. Then, shape this mixture into 1-inch meatballs.
3. Place meatballs in a shallow roasting pan and bake them for 16 minutes or until they are browned. Transfer meatballs to the slow cooker.
4. In another mixing bowl, vigorously combine the remaining ingredients, along with the remaining ketchup. Pour the mixture over the meatballs in the slow cooker.
5. Cover and cook on Low setting for 4 hours 30 minutes. Enjoy!

– BEEF –

78. Ricotta and Beef Dip

You can make a restaurant-quality dipping sauce in your slow cooker by simply mixing the right ingredients and let them cook gently and slowly.

Ready in about
2 hours
40 minutes

NUTRITIONAL INFORMATION
(Per Serving)

71 - Calories
5g - Fat
2.6g - Carbs
4g - Protein
0.7g - Sugars

Ingredients

- 1/2 teaspoon hot pepper sauce
- 2 ounces Ricotta cheese, softened
- 1/2 tablespoon water
- 2 tablespoons of sour cream
- 1/2 teaspoon Worcestershire sauce
- 4 ounces canned condensed chili beef soup
- 1/4 teaspoon chili sauce

Directions

1. In your slow cooker, combine all ingredients; mix until everything is well combined.
2. Cover and cook on Low for 2 hours 30 minutes, stirring periodically.
3. Serve warm with your favorite dippers such as corn tortilla, crackers or breadsticks.

– BEEF –

79. Hot Mexican-Style Beef Dip

Extremely rich and sophisticated, with a dash of high-quality herbs, this is not an entry-level meat dip. Serve with tortilla strips, corn chips and pieces of pita. Enjoy!

Ready in about
1 hours
40 minutes

NUTRITIONAL
INFORMATION
(Per Serving)

223 - Calories
18.3g - Fat
4.3g - Carbs
10.3g - Protein
2.9g - Sugars

Ingredients

- 1/2 teaspoon chipotle pepper, finely minced
- 1 canned tomato, drained
- 1/2 pound beef sausage
- 2 tablespoons picante sauce
- 1/2 cup Asadero cheese

Directions

1. Brown the sausage in a nonstick skillet over medium heat; crumble it and discard the excess fat. Transfer the crumbled sausage to the slow cooker.
2. Next, add the remaining ingredients to the cooker and simmer the mixture on Low for 1 hour 30 minutes.

– BEEF –

80. Barbecued Beef and Bean Soup

Slow cooking is a fantastic method for preparing holiday soup recipes. Great Northern beans are available year-round but you can use any white beans in this recipe.

Ready in about 9 hours 20 minutes

NUTRITIONAL INFORMATION
(Per Serving)

363 - Calories
7g - Fat
43.3g - Carbs
31.1g - Protein
10.4g - Sugars

Ingredients

- f short ribs
- 1/2 tablespoon balsamic vinegar
- 1/4 cup barbecue sauce
- 1/2 cup beef stock
- 1/2 cup water
- 1 clove garlic, finely minced
- 1/2 teaspoon sea salt
- 1/2 teaspoon freshly cracked black pepper
- 1 cup Great Northern beans, soaked
- 1/2 red onion, finely chopped

Directions

1. Add all ingredients to your slow cooker, except for barbecue sauce.
2. Cover with the lid and cook on Low heat setting for 9 hours.
3. After that, discard the short ribs; cut meat from bones. Return meat to the slow cooker. Add barbecue sauce just before serving. Serve and enjoy!

– BEEF –

81. Festive Beef Meatballs

Looking for an easy holiday recipe? This recipe is both delicious and unique! Aromatic onion soup mix brings the magic into your everyday cooking!

Ready in about 50 minutes

NUTRITIONAL INFORMATION
(Per Serving)

370 - Calories
16.3g - Fat
32.7g - Carbs
24.7g - Protein
26.5g - Sugars

Ingredients

- 1/2 envelope dry onion soup mix
- 1 teaspoon Worcestershire sauce
- 1 cup ground beef
- 1/4 cup evaporated milk

For the Sauce:
- 2 tablespoons brown sugar, packed
- 1/2 cup ketchup
- 1/2 tablespoon soy sauce

Directions

1. Combine the ground beef, Worcestershire sauce, evaporated milk, and soup mix. Shape the mixture into 8 balls.
2. Broil the meatballs for 15 minutes, turning once or twice to keep them from burning.
3. Mix the sauce ingredients in your slow cooker; add the meatballs and cook for 30 minutes.
4. Serve and enjoy!

– BEEF –

82. Sunday Hamburger Dip

The slow cooker is an amazing kitchen "companion". Slow cooked hamburger dip is a flavorful and memorable recipe. It also frees up your oven and stove for other recipes. Win-win!

Ready in about
2 hours
40 minutes

NUTRITIONAL INFORMATION
(Per Serving)

376 - Calories
16.9g - Fat
14.7g - Carbs
40.9g - Protein
5.7g - Sugars

Ingredients

- 1/2 cup shallots, chopped
- 2 tablespoons tomato ketchup
- 1/2 teaspoon dried oregano
- 1/2 teaspoon sea salt
- 1/2 teaspoon dried rosemary
- 1/2 teaspoon dried basil
- 2 ounces canned tomato sauce
- 1/2 teaspoon white sugar
- 1/2 cup ground pork
- 1 cup ground beef
- 2 ounces cream cheese, softened
- 1 clove garlic, minced

Directions

1. In a nonstick skillet, brown ground meat along with shallot and garlic. Transfer the meat mixture to your slow cooker.
2. Add the rest of the above ingredients.
3. Set your cooker on Low and simmer the mixture until everything is thoroughly blended, approximately 2 hours 30 minutes.
4. Now, taste and adjust the seasonings. Serve with tortilla chips, if desired.

– BEEF –

83. The Best Christmas Steak Ever

(Preparing chuck steak in a slow cooker has a number of advantages to the traditional methods of searing or grilling. See it for yourself!

Ready in about
5 hours
40 minutes

NUTRITIONAL INFORMATION
(Per Serving)

331 - Calories
15.1g - Fat
10.1g - Carbs
36.8g - Protein
7g - Sugars

Ingredients

- 1/4 cup tomato paste
- 1 tablespoon Worcestershire sauce
- 1/2 teaspoon garlic, finely minced
- 1/2 teaspoon honey
- 1/2 teaspoon dried dill weed
- 1/2 teaspoon dried rosemary, crushed
- 1/2 teaspoon kosher salt
- 1/2 teaspoon smoked cayenne powder
- 1/4 teaspoon ground black pepper
- 1/2 teaspoon dried sage, crushed
- 1/4 teaspoon dried basil
- 1/2 pound chuck steak, boneless and sliced
- 2 tablespoons apple cider vinegar

Directions

1. Lay the beef on the bottom of your slow cooker.
2. In a small-sized mixing dish, combine the remaining items. Pour the mixture over the meat; toss to coat well.
3. Cover and cook on Low for 5 hours 30 minutes. Serve over baked beans, if desired.

– BEEF –

84. Cheesy Beef with Sweet Corn

You're about to cook the best beef with corn you've ever eaten! This is one of the favorite potluck recipes.

Ready in about 5 hours

NUTRITIONAL INFORMATION
(Per Serving)

493 - Calories
27.8g - Fat
20.6g - Carbs
41.9g - Protein
4.2g Sugars

Ingredients

- 4 ounces sweet corn
- 2 ounces tomato
- 1 cup beef, minced
- 2 ounces Cottage cheese
- 1/4 cup scallions, finely chopped
- 1/4 teaspoon sea salt, or more to your liking
- 1/2 teaspoon garlic, minced
- 2 ounces Swiss cheese, shredded
- 1/4 cup beef broth
- 1 tablespoon olive oil
- 2 ounces sour cream
- 1/4 teaspoon freshly ground black pepper

Directions

1. Heat olive oil in your slow cooker over a medium flame.
2. Brown the beef for 6 minutes, stirring and crumbling it occasionally. Now, stir in the remaining ingredients, except for sweet corn. Adjust the seasonings and seal the slow cooker.
3. Then, cook for 3 hours 30 minutes on Low. Then, add sweet corn and continue simmering for 1 hour more.
4. Once the time is up, open the slow cooker and divide the mixture among six serving bowls. Enjoy!

– BEEF –

85. Dinner Beef and Pork Chili

This amazing chili is perfect for entertaining. Get your friend or kids involved: One can chop the veggies while another can sauté the ingredients. Cooking is fun!

Ready in about 8 hours 15 minutes

NUTRITIONAL INFORMATION (Per Serving)

330 - Calories
15.5g - Fat
28g - Carbs
24g - Protein
12.8g - Sugars

Ingredients

- 8 ounces canned tomato sauce
- 1/2 cup ground lean beef
- 1 cup ground lean pork
- 1 stalk celery, chopped
- 1/4 cup green onion, diced
- 1 tablespoon chili powder
- 1 green garlic, finely chopped
- 1/2 cup parsnip, chopped
- 1/2 cup green chilies, finely chopped
- 1/2 bell pepper, seeded and diced
- 1/2 teaspoon oregano, finely minced
- 1/2 teaspoon adobo sauce
- 1 teaspoon fresh basil, finely minced
- 1 tablespoon olive oil
- 1/2 teaspoon salt, or more to taste

Directions

1. First, heat the oil over medium-high flame. Sauté the pepper with green onion and garlic in hot oil for 4 minutes.
2. Then, throw in the pork, beef, parsnip and celery; cook for 4 minutes longer or until they're lightly browned.
3. Stir in the rest of the items, cover, and cook for 8 hours on Low. Serve warm and enjoy!

86. Beef and Zucchini Loaf

A slow cooked meat and zucchini loaf is a classic that you must try. Slow cooking is one of the best cooking methods to achieve flavors and textures that will blow you away!

Ready in about 6 hours 40 minutes

NUTRITIONAL INFORMATION
(Per Serving)

377 - Calories
17.2g - Fat
12.3g - Carbs
43.9g - Protein
7.4g - Sugars

Ingredients

- 2 tablespoons Mozzarella cheese, shredded
- 1/4 cup Parmigiano-Reggiano, grated
- 1 whole egg
- 1 tablespoon apple cider vinegar
- 1/4 teaspoon ground black pepper
- 1/2 teaspoon dried basil
- 1/4 teaspoon salt, or more to taste
- 1/2 teaspoon dried oregano
- 1 green garlic, minced
- 1 cup lean beef, ground
- 2 tablespoons hot spicy tomato ketchup
- 1/2 small-sized onion, minced
- 1/2 cup zucchini, shredded

Directions

1. Combine all ingredients, except for the ketchup and Mozzarella, in a large-sized mixing bowl. Now, mix them thoroughly and shape them into a loaf.
2. Next, line the bottom of a slow cooker with foil; spray foil with a nonstick cooking spray.
3. Place the meatloaf on foil; top with ketchup and Mozzarella.
4. Cover the slow cooker and cook for 6 hours 30 minutes on Low.

– BEEF –

87. Smoky Beef Chili

Here is a simple way to make chili; you can add your favorite combo of spices as well. Great with rich, crispy salad.

Ready in about
9 hours
20 minutes

NUTRITIONAL INFORMATION
(Per Serving)

425 - Calories
3.7g - Fat
64.3g - Carbs
34.9g - Protein
3.4g - Sugars

Ingredients

- 8 ounces canned fire-roasted tomatoes, diced
- 1 clove garlic, minced
- 1/2 teaspoon smoked paprika
- 1 chipotle chile in adobo, chopped
- 1/2 teaspoon smoked cayenne pepper
- 1/2 teaspoon hot paprika
- 1/2 teaspoon ground bay leaf
- 1/2 medium shallot, diced
- 1 cup ground beef
- 10 ounces canned kidney beans, drained and rinsed

Directions

1. In a saucepan, sauté the beef until it's just browned. Drain and replace to the slow cooker.
2. Then, throw in the remaining ingredients. Cook on Low for 9 hours. Serve right away.

– BEEF –

88. Christmas Dinner Beef Roast

If you're looking for a festive beef roast recipe that is easy to make, look no further! Thanks to the slow cooker, you can have the restaurant-style roast at your own home.

Ready in about
7 hours
40 minutes

NUTRITIONAL INFORMATION
(Per Serving)

269 - Calories
13.5g - Fat
9.7g - Carbs
24.4g - Protein
4.6g - Sugars

Ingredients

- 1 tablespoon olive oil
- 1/2 pound top round beef roast
- 1 ½ tablespoons apple cider vinegar
- 1/2 red onion, sliced into rings
- 1/4 cup water
- 1/2 tablespoon smoked cayenne pepper
- 1/2 teaspoon onion powder
- 1/4 teaspoon ground black pepper
- 1/2 teaspoon garlic powder
- 1/2 teaspoon smoked paprika
- 1/2 teaspoon dried thyme
- 1/4 teaspoon salt
- 1/2 teaspoon dried marjoram
- 1/3 cup beef broth, preferably homemade
- 1/2 cup tomato puree

Directions

1. In a small-sized mixing bowl, combine smoked cayenne pepper, paprika, thyme, marjoram, onion powder, garlic powder, black pepper, and salt. Mix to combine well.
2. Rub this spice mixture all over your meat.
3. Then, warm olive oil in a sauté pan over medium flame. Sear the roast for about 5 minutes on each side.
4. Treat the inside of the slow cooker with a shortening. Lay the onion rings on the bottom of your slow cooker; place seared meat on the onions.
5. In a mixing dish, combine the tomato puree, water, vinegar, and broth. Now, pour the mixture into your slow cooker.
6. Now, seal the cooker and cook for 7 hours 30 minutes on Low heat setting.

– BEEF –

89. Beef Roast with Mushrooms and Leeks

Slow cooking ensures you get moist and tender beef roast without losing any nutrition and flavor from the meat.

Mound fresh salad on a serving plate. Top with warm beef roast and enjoy!

Ready in about
7 hours
40 minutes

NUTRITIONAL
INFORMATION
(Per Serving)

367 - Calories
27.4g - Fat
5.3g - Carbs
25g - Protein
1.9g - Sugars

Ingredients

- 1/4 cup water
- 1/2 cup porcini mushrooms, sliced
- 1/2 pound beef chuck roast
- 1/2 teaspoon garlic powder
- 1/3 teaspoon black pepper
- 1/2 teaspoon crushed rosemary, dried
- 1/4 teaspoon salt
- 1/2 teaspoon dried oregano
- 1/2 tablespoon Dijon mustard
- 1/4 cup leeks, chopped
- 1/2 tablespoon lard

Directions

1. Melt the lard in a heavy skillet over medium-high flame.
2. In a mixing dish, combine together the rosemary, oregano, garlic powder, black pepper, and salt. Now, rub the spice mixture onto the roast.
3. Now, sear the roast about 6 minutes per side. Transfer seared beef to the slow cooker that are set on Low. Add the remaining ingredients.
4. Cook approximately 7 hours 30 minutes and don't lift the lid too much. Bon appétit!

– BEEF –

90. Meatballs in Barbecue Sauce

You can't go wrong with slow-cooked and well-seasoned meatballs in sauce. These meatballs are cooked gently over 5 hours and served warm with lots of salad.

Ready in about
5 hours
40 minutes

NUTRITIONAL INFORMATION
(Per Serving)

531 - Calories
12g - Fat
60.3g - Carbs
45.8g - Protein
23.6g - Sugars

Ingredients

For the Meatballs:
- 1 egg
- 1/2 cup bread crumbs
- 1/2 teaspoon garlic powder
- 1/2 pound beef, ground
- 1/2 package onion soup mix

For the Sauce:
- 1/4 cup sweet pickle relish
- 1/2 tablespoon dry mustard
- 1/2 teaspoon salt
- 1/3 teaspoon ground black pepper
- 1/4 teaspoon red pepper flakes, crushed
- 2 tablespoons red wine vinegar
- 1 tablespoon brown sugar
- 1/4 cup vegetable stock
- 1 onion, finely chopped
- 1 clove garlic, minced
- 1/2 can tomato paste

Directions

1. Combine all ingredients for the meatballs; mix until everything is well incorporated. Shape the mixture into 8 meatballs.
2. Then, brown the meatballs in a nonstick skillet that is lightly greased with 1/2 tablespoon of olive oil.
3. Next, stir all sauce ingredients into the slow cooker; stir well to combine.
4. Throw in browned meatballs, and slow cook, covered, for 5 hours 30 minutes on Low. Serve with baked potatoes or hamburger buns. Bon appétit!

FISH & SEAFOOD

– FISH & SEAFOOD –

91. Baby Potato and Seafood Stew

A well-prepared seafood stew is a royal meal! To make this recipe's nutritional profile, we used mussel meats, king prawns and squid rings. You can use your favorite seafood mix and achieve great results as well.

Ready in about
6 hours
20 minutes

NUTRITIONAL INFORMATION
(Per Serving)

313 - Calories
5g - Fat
26.5g - Carbs
41.5g - Protein
5.6g - Sugars

Ingredients

- 1/2 pound baby potatoes, quartered
- 1 clove garlic, minced
- 2 cups vegetable broth
- 1/4 teaspoon ground black pepper, or more to your liking
- 1/2 teaspoon dried basil
- 1/2 teaspoon salt
- 1/2 tablespoon fresh cilantro
- 12 ounces canned tomatoes, crushed
- 1 pound mixed seafood
- 1 green onion, chopped
- 1/2 tablespoon apple cider vinegar

Directions

1. Simply throw all of the above ingredients, except for the seafood, into your slow cooker; gently stir to combine.
2. Cover and cook for 5 hours 30 minutes on Low heat setting.
3. Afterwards, stir in the seafood; let it cook for 40 minutes longer; serve immediately.

— FISH & SEAFOOD —

92. Seafood and Tomato Chowder

There are many health benefits of eating seafood. They are sources of essential nutrients such as B-complex vitamins, vitamin A, vitamin D, protein, and omega-3 fatty acid. Seafood fights against depression and boosts our immune system and brainpower.

Ready in about 8 hours

NUTRITIONAL INFORMATION
(Per Serving)

202 - Calories
1.7g - Fat
22.5g - Carbs
25.5g - Protein
10.9g - Sugars

Ingredients

- 1 clove garlic, minced
- 3 ounces lobster meat
- 3 ounces diced cooked clams
- 3 ounces peeled raw shrimp
- 1/2 carrot, chopped
- 1/2 teaspoon balsamic vinegar
- 1/2 stalk celery, diced
- 6 ounces canned diced tomatoes
- 1 tablespoon fresh chives, chopped
- 5 ounces clam juice
- 3 ounces tomato paste
- 1/2 onion, chopped
- Lemon slices, for garnish
- 1 tablespoon minced fresh Italian parsley

Directions

1. Place all of the above ingredients, except seafood, chives and lemon slices, in your slow cooker
2. Stir vigorously until everything is well incorporated. Cook on Low heat setting for 7 hours.
3. Add the seafood and chives; cook on High for 40 minutes. Serve with lemon slices.

– FISH & SEAFOOD –

93. Crab and Mayo Dip

This classic dipping sauce makes a great spring snack or dinner! Serve with naan and lots of salad if desired.

Ready in about
5 hours
40 minutes

NUTRITIONAL INFORMATION
(Per Serving)

161 - Calories
5.5g - Fat
9.4g - Carbs
15.4g - Protein
3.9g - Sugars

Ingredients

- 2 ounces Cottage cheese
- 1/2 tablespoon horseradish sauce
- 2 tablespoons fish broth
- 1/2 tablespoon Worcestershire sauce
- 1/4 cup carrot, chopped
- 6 ounces crab meat
- 1/2 tablespoon orange juice
- 1/2 teaspoon cilantro, finely chopped
- Salt, to your liking
- 1 tablespoon mayonnaise
- 1/2 cup bell pepper, seeded and diced

Directions

1. Place all of the above ingredients in your slow cooker; cook for 5 hours 30 minutes on Low.
2. Once the time is up, serve warm with your favorite dippers.

– FISH & SEAFOOD –

94. Shrimp, Peppers, and Cheese Dip

For this rich and satisfying dip, two kinds of cheese are melted gently and tossed with seasonings and shrimp – a winning combination!

Ready in about
1 hour
50 minutes

NUTRITIONAL INFORMATION
(Per Serving)

275 - Calories
21.2g - Fat
4.3g - Carbs
15g - Protein
2.5g - Sugars

Ingredients

- 1/2 cup shrimp, chopped
- 1/4 cup scallions, sliced
- 1/2 teaspoon sea salt
- 2 tablespoons sour cream
- 1/4 teaspoon ground black pepper
- 1/2 teaspoon lemon juice
- 1/4 cup Pecorino Romano, grated
- 1/4 cup cream cheese, room temperature
- 1/2 teaspoon cayenne pepper
- 1/2 teaspoon Dijon mustard
- 1/4 cup roasted red pepper, chopped

Directions

1. Melt the cheeses in your slow cooker approximately 35 minutes; make sure to stir continuously.
2. Then, add the rest of the above ingredients; cook for 1 hour 10 minutes longer.
3. Serve with dippers of choice.

– FISH & SEAFOOD –

95. Tomato and Seafood Stew

This aromatic and rich stew is true comfort in a bowl. You can spice it up and add your favorite hot spices like Berbere, Aleppo pepper, chili powder, and Harissa. Serve with a crusty sourdough bread.

Ready in about 6 hours 30 minutes

NUTRITIONAL INFORMATION (Per Serving)

275 - Calories
3.8g - Fat
18.5g - Carbs
39.4g - Protein
8.5g - Sugars

Ingredients

- 1 pound mixed seafood
- 2 cups roasted vegetable stock
- 1/2 teaspoon parsley
- 6 ounces crushed tomatoes
- 1 clove garlic, minced
- 1 carrot, cut into coins
- Salt and crushed red pepper flakes, to your liking
- 2 tablespoons white wine
- 1/2 yellow onion, chopped

Directions

1. Arrange all of the ingredients, except the seafood, in your slow cooker.
2. Then, cover with the lid and slow cook for 5 hours 30 minutes on Low setting.
3. Stir in the seafood; let it cook an additional 50 minutes on Low setting. Serve hot with garlic croutons, if desired.

– FISH & SEAFOOD –

96. Potato, Corn and Shrimp Chowder

Here's a stress-free seafood recipe that may become your favorite! In this recipe, you can use pickled jalapeño peppers to enhance the flavor of your chowder.

Ready in about
6 hours
30 minutes

NUTRITIONAL INFORMATION
(Per Serving)

418 - Calories
9.7g - Fat
57.8g - Carbs
28.3g - Protein
7g - Sugars

Ingredients

- 6 ounces shrimp, peeled
- 4 ounces green beans
- 1/4 teaspoon ground black pepper
- 1/4 teaspoon salt, or more to your liking
- 1/4 teaspoon cayenne pepper
- 2 small-sized potatoes, quartered
- 2 tablespoons flour
- 2 cups chicken broth
- 1/4 cup heavy cream
- 4 ounces sweet corn

Directions

1. Whisk the broth and flour in a mixing dish. Then, add the mixture to the slow cooker. Now, add green beans, sweet corn, and potatoes.
2. Cover the slow cooker; cook for 5 hours 30 minutes on Low; stir in the heavy cream and shrimp; cook an additional 50 minutes on Low setting.
3. Season with black pepper, cayenne pepper, and salt. Serve warm and enjoy!

– FISH & SEAFOOD –

97. Shrimp with Potato and Corn

Looking for creative ways to cook with shrimp? This chunky soup is both healthy and gourmet. Enjoy!

Ready in about
3 hours
40 minutes

NUTRITIONAL
INFORMATION
(Per Serving)

367 - Calories
4.2g - Fat
53.1g - Carbs
33.5g - Protein
8.6g - Sugars

Ingredients

- 1 tablespoon clam juice
- 1 tablespoon Cajun seasoning
- 1/2 teaspoon black peppercorns
- 1 small-sized onion, thinly sliced
- 1/2 teaspoon mustard seeds
- 2 ears corn, halved
- Water, as needed
- 1/2 pound baby red skin potatoes
- 1/2 pound shrimp
- 1 clove garlic, finely minced

Directions

1. Place the potatoes, corn, Cajun seasoning, mustard seeds, peppercorns, onions, and cloves garlic in your slow cooker. Pour in the clam juice and water.
2. Cook on High setting for 3 hours or until the vegetables are tender. Add the shrimp and continue to cook for a further 30 minutes on High setting. Serve warm and enjoy!

– FISH & SEAFOOD –

98. Salmon and Zucchini Soup

A light and satisfying, this fish soup is guaranteed to make your meals so much better. Serve this as a light lunch on a brisk and rainy autumn days.

Ready in about
2 hours
10 minutes

NUTRITIONAL INFORMATION
(Per Serving)

107 - Calories
3g - Fat
10.3g - Carbs
11.6g - Protein
1.9g - Sugars

Ingredients

- 1 clove garlic, minced
- 1 tablespoon soy sauce
- 1/2 shallot, sliced
- 1 zucchini, thinly sliced
- 1/2 salmon fillet
- Fresh chopped cilantro, for garnish
- 1/2 cup kale leaves, torn into pieces

Directions

1. Lay salmon fillet on the bottom of your slow cooker. Cover salmon fillets with water; slow cook on High for 1 hour 10 minutes.
2. Add the remaining ingredients, except the cilantro. Cook for 50 minutes more or until heated through.
3. Ladle the soup into individual bowls and garnish with fresh cilantro. Enjoy!

– FISH & SEAFOOD –

99. Tilapia Fillets with Kale

In this recipe, you can substitute regular onions with the shallots. Serve with steamed kale and miso sauce if desired.

Ready in about 2 hours 40 minutes

NUTRITIONAL INFORMATION
(Per Serving)

116 - Calories
1.3g - Fat
5.6g - Carbs
21.8g - Protein
1.6g - Sugars

Ingredients

- 1/2 teaspoon cayenne pepper
- 1 teaspoon salt
- 1/2 teaspoon freshly ground black pepper
- 1/2 lime, freshly squeezed
- 2 tilapia fillets
- 1/4 teaspoon shallot powder
- 1 garlic clove, chopped
- 1/4 teaspoon dried mustard
- 1/2 onion, sliced

Directions

1. Rub fish fillets with cayenne pepper, shallot powder, salt, and ground black pepper. Place tilapia fillets in the center of a piece of aluminum foil. Lay the onions and garlic on the fish fillets.
2. Drizzle lime juice over all; add the mustard.
3. Fold the foil over the fish and vegetables so everything is sealed up. Lay the packets in the slow cooker.
4. Now, seal your slow cooker and heat on High; slow cook for 2 hours 30 minutes. Bon appétit!

– FISH & SEAFOOD –

100. Shrimp and Corn Chowder

If you love chowders, the slow cooker is a great tool to prepare this all-in-one meal while saving you time and money. You can add chopped smoked ham to enrich the flavors. Bon appétit!

Ready in about
6 hours
40 minutes

NUTRITIONAL INFORMATION
(Per Serving)

368 - Calories
9.6g - Fat
39g - Carbs
32.3g - Protein
6.5g - Sugars

Ingredients

- 6 ounces shrimp, peeled
- 2 baby potatoes, quartered
- 2 cups chicken broth
- 4 ounces green peas
- 3 tablespoons all-purpose flour
- 1/4 cup heavy cream
- 4 ounces sweet corn
- Salt and freshly cracked black pepper, to your liking

Directions

1. First, whisk the flour and chicken broth in a mixing dish. Transfer the mixture to the slow cooker.
2. Stir in the remaining ingredients, except the cream and shrimp.
3. Seal your slow cooker according to the manufacturer's instructions; cook the chowder for 5 hours 30 minutes on Low heat setting.
4. Next, stir in the heavy cream and shrimp; cook an additional 50 minutes on Low. Serve warm.

VEGAN

– VEGAN –

101. Vegan Sweet Farro

Farro is an ancient grain that has a lot of health benefits. It reduces the risk of asthma, stroke and diabetes. Farro also prevents numerous inflammatory diseases, constipation, and obesity.

Ready in about
2 hours
40 minutes

NUTRITIONAL INFORMATION
(Per Serving)

303 - Calories
9.7g - Fat
47.5g - Carbs
7.5g - Protein
7.8g - Sugars

Ingredients

- 1 cup farro, rinsed
- 2 cups water
- 1/2 cup coconut water
- 1/8 teaspoon sea salt
- 1/2 teaspoon pure vanilla essence
- 1/2 teaspoon cinnamon powder
- 1/2 teaspoon ground cloves
- 1/4 teaspoon ground anise seeds
- 1 tablespoon maple syrup
- 1/4 cup coarsely chopped walnut, for garnish

Directions

1. Simply add all of the above items, except walnuts, to your slow cooker. Cover with the lid, and cook for 2 hours 30 minutes on High.
2. Meanwhile, in a nonstick skillet, toast the walnuts until they're fragrant and lightly browned.
3. Lastly, serve your farro in individual serving bowls, sprinkled with toasted walnuts. Bon appétit!

– VEGAN –

102. Vegan Miso Soup

Here's a million-dollar soup you will crave during windy autumn days! Press your tofu before adding it to the slow cooker. Set some heavy object on top and let it stand at least 30 minutes.

Ready in about 8 hours

NUTRITIONAL INFORMATION
(Per Serving)

67 - Calories
3g - Fat
5.3g - Carbs
6.3g - Protein
1.5g - Sugars

Ingredients

- 4 ounces firm tofu, diced
- 1/2 cup scallions, diced
- 1 tablespoon miso paste
- 3 cups water
- 1/2 cup spinach, torn into pieces

Directions

1. Pour the water into your slow cooker. Stir in the miso paste; whisk until it is dissolved.
2. Next, add the tofu and cook on Low heat setting for 7 hours 30 minutes.
3. Add the scallions and spinach, turn the heat to High, and cook an additional 20 minutes. Stir before serving and enjoy!

– VEGAN –

103. Vegan Apple and Pear Pudding

Looking for a last-minute recipe to satisfy your sweet tooth? This stunning fruit pudding will fit the bill! You can add golden raisins if desired.

Ready in about
2 hours
40 minutes

NUTRITIONAL INFORMATION
(Per Serving)

537 - Calories
25.6g - Fat
68.6g - Carbs
7.8g - Protein
49.9g - Sugars

Ingredients

- 1/4 cup almonds, finely chopped
- 1 cup stale whole-wheat bread
- 1/2 cup almond milk
- 1/2 tablespoon ground flaxseeds mixed with 1 tablespoon warm water
- 1/2 teaspoon pure almond extract
- 1/3 cup sugar
- 1/2 cup pears, peeled, cored and chopped
- 1/4 teaspoon pure vanilla extract
- 1/2 cup apples, peeled, cored and chopped
- 3 tablespoons vegan chocolate chips
- 1 tablespoon apple brandy
- Nonstick cooking spray (butter flavor)

Directions

1. Lightly oil your slow cooker with a nonstick spray.
2. In a bowl, place the pears, apples, stale bread, almond milk, apple brandy, flaxseed mixture, and sugar. Stir until everything is well combined.
3. Stir in the remaining ingredients; scrape the mixture into your slow cooker. Cook on High setting approximately 2 hours 30 minutes. Serve at room temperature.

– VEGAN –

104. Powerful Wheat Berry Breakfast

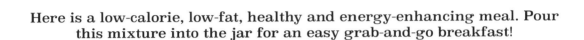

Here is a low-calorie, low-fat, healthy and energy-enhancing meal. Pour this mixture into the jar for an easy grab-and-go breakfast!

Ready in about
9 hours
15 minutes

NUTRITIONAL INFORMATION
(Per Serving)

74 - Calories
0.3g - Fat
16.7g - Carbs
2.4g - Protein
0.3g - Sugars

Ingredients

- 1/4 teaspoon pure vanilla essence
- 1/2 cup wheat berries
- 1 ½ cups water
- 2 tablespoons dried black currants
- 1/4 teaspoon cinnamon powder

Directions

1. Add all ingredients to the slow cooker. Stir to combine and distribute ingredients.
2. Cook for 9 hours on Low setting.
3. Stir before serving and enjoy.

– VEGAN –

105. Multigrain Cereal with Golden Raisins

Light and delicious, this cereal breakfast is an ideal meal to munch on when you're on the go! If golden raisins aren't your cup of tea, try adding your favorite dried fruits.

Ready in about
7 hours
40 minutes

NUTRITIONAL INFORMATION
(Per Serving)

149 - Calories
1.7g - Fat
31.8g - Carbs
3.8g - Protein
11.1g - Sugars

Ingredients

- 2 cups water
- 1/2 teaspoon grated nutmeg
- 2 tablespoons wheat berries
- 1/4 cup golden raisins
- 1/2 cup rolled oats
- 1/2 teaspoon ground cinnamon

Directions

1. Simply drop all of the above ingredients in your slow cooker. Stir until everything's well combined.
2. Cook for 7 hours 30 minutes on Low. Stir and serve warm.

– VEGAN –

106. Morning Quinoa with Berries

Quinoa is a superfood that has a lot of proven health benefits. In this recipe, you can use red or white quinoa, it is totally up to you.

Ready in about
2 hours
40 minutes

NUTRITIONAL INFORMATION
(Per Serving)

220 - Calories
2.9g - Fat
43.2g - Carbs
6.5g - Protein
7.9g - Sugars

Ingredients

- 1/2 apple, thinly sliced
- 1/4 teaspoon crystallized ginger
- 2 tablespoons dried cherries
- 3 tablespoons dried apricots, chopped
- 1/2 cup quinoa
- 1/4 teaspoon ground cloves
- 1/2 teaspoon ground cinnamon
- A dash of grated nutmeg
- 1 cup water
- 1/2 teaspoon dark brown sugar

Directions

1. Place all ingredients in your slow cooker. Stir to combine well.
2. Slow cook on High for 2 hours 30 minutes.

– VEGAN –

107. Aromatic Fig Spread

Thanks to its amazing technology, a slow cooker will take your spreads from "blah" to "yippee"! In this recipe, you can substitute a fresh ginger for crystallized one.

Ready in about
6 hours
15 minutes

NUTRITIONAL INFORMATION
(Per Serving)

359 - Calories
1.2g - Fat
91.4g - Carbs
4g - Protein
72.2g - Sugars

Ingredients

- 1/2 tablespoon fresh ginger, grated
- 1/4 cup brown sugar
- 1/2 pound figs
- 1/8 teaspoon grated nutmeg
- 1/4 cup water
- 1/4 teaspoon cinnamon powder
- 1 tablespoon lemon juice

Directions

1. Place all ingredients in your slow cooker. Stir to combine. Cook on Low for 3 hours 30 minutes.
2. Remove the lid and cook for 2 hours 30 minutes more or until the mixture is thickened.
3. Transfer to the airtight containers; refrigerate up to 6 weeks.

– VEGAN –

108. Winter Vegetable Chowder

Delicious and filling, a hot bowl of vegetable chowder is sure to warm the soul, no matter what the season. This combination of veggies has a great flavor and soft texture, which makes it perfect for a thick and satisfying chowder.

Ready in about
6 hours
10 minutes

NUTRITIONAL INFORMATION
(Per Serving)

112 - Calories
0.7g - Fat
24g - Carbs
5.9g - Protein
8.3g - Sugars

Ingredients

- 1/4 pound cauliflower florets
- 1/2 onion, chopped
- 1/2 parsnip, cut into coins
- 1/2 pound broccoli florets
- 1 carrot, cut into coins
- 2 cups vegetable stock
- 1/2 stalk celery, diced
- 1 clove garlic, minced
- 1/2 teaspoon ground black pepper
- 1/4 teaspoon dried dill weed
- 1/4 teaspoon kosher salt

Directions

1. Place the broccoli, cauliflower, stock, onions, garlic, salt, black pepper, dill weed in your slow cooker. Stir to combine well.
2. Add the remaining vegetables; cook on Low for 5 hours 30 minutes or until the vegetables are fork tender.
3. Purée the mixture with an immersion blender until everything is well combined.
4. Cook on Low for 20 minutes more. Serve warm.

– VEGAN –

109. Cannellini Beans with Porcini Mushrooms

Who said beans have to be boring? Cannellini beans are a great protein source and a staple of a vegan diet. If you don't have chervil on hand, a great substitute would be fresh parsley.

Ready in about
9 hours
30 minutes

NUTRITIONAL
INFORMATION
(Per Serving)

385 - Calories
7.4g - Fat
65.6g - Carbs
12g - Protein
6.6g - Sugars

Ingredients

- 1 tablespoon olive oil
- 1 clove garlic, finely minced
- 2 tablespoons dried porcini mushrooms
- Sea salt and freshly ground black pepper, to your liking
- 1/2 stalk celery, diced
- 1 carrot, diced
- 1/4 teaspoon fennel seeds
- 1/2 onion, chopped
- 1/2 teaspoon chervil
- 1 cup boiling water
- 1/2 pound dried cannellini beans
- 1 cup roasted vegetable stock
- 1 parsnip, diced

Directions

1. The night before, place the beans in your slow cooker. Fill the cooker with boiling water and soak overnight.
2. Drain the beans. Pour the boiling water over the mushrooms; soak for 20 minutes.
3. Warm the oil in a nonstick skillet over medium heat. Now, sauté the onions, garlic, celery, parsnips, and carrots.
4. Sauté for a few minutes; add the sautéed vegetables to the slow cooker; stir in the rest of the above ingredients.
5. Stir in the soaked mushrooms and cook on Low for 9 hours. Serve and enjoy!

– VEGAN –

110. Sunrise Family Farro

Simple and tasty, this dish is perfect for your next dinner. The combo of farro and seasonings has never tasted better!

Ready in about
2 hours
40 minutes

NUTRITIONAL INFORMATION
(Per Serving)

284 - Calories
2.6g - Fat
54.4g - Carbs
14.3g - Protein
1g - Sugars

Ingredients

- 2 cups vegetable broth
- Salt and freshly ground black pepper, to your liking
- 1/2 cup water
- 1/4 teaspoon cayenne pepper
- 1 cup farro

Directions

1. First, rinse farro with cold water; add rinsed farro to the slow cooker.
2. Then, pour in the broth and water. Cover the slow cooker and cook on High for 2 hours 30 minutes.
3. Season with salt, ground black pepper, and cayenne pepper. Serve right away and enjoy!

– VEGAN –

111. Light Potato and Leek Purée

Here's one of the best winter-worthy puree recipes that is chock full of vitamin-packed vegetables and aromatic seasonings. Sangiovese-based wine goes well for this recipe.

Ready in about
6 hours
40 minutes

NUTRITIONAL INFORMATION
(Per Serving)

251 - Calories
1.8g - Fat
49.8g - Carbs
9.8g - Protein
8g - Sugars

Ingredients

- 2 cups roasted-vegetable broth
- 1/2 parsnip, sliced
- 1 carrot, diced
- 1/4 teaspoon freshly cracked black pepper
- 2 Russet potatoes, peeled and cubed
- 1/2 teaspoon salt
- 1 cup sliced leeks

Directions

1. Stir all ingredients into your slow cooker. Stir using a spoon until everything is combined well.
2. Cook on Low for 6 hours 30 minutes.
3. Purée the mixture with an immersion blender. Serve hot.

– VEGAN –

112. Easy Squash Chili

High-quality beans, vegetables and carefully selected spices are magically transformed into a hearty squash chili that is healthy as well. This recipe is both easy and sophisticated. Bon appétit!

Ready in about
8 hours
20 minutes

NUTRITIONAL INFORMATION
(Per Serving)

120 - Calories
0.8g - Fat
28.1g - Carbs
4.8g - Protein
7.8g - Sugars

Ingredients

- 8 ounces canned red beans, drained and rinsed
- 1/2 teaspoon liquid smoke
- 10 ounces canned tomatoes, diced
- 1/2 stalk celery, diced
- 1/2 yellow onion, diced
- 1/2 teaspoon garlic, minced
- 1/4 cup fresh corn kernels
- 1/2 tablespoon hot sauce
- 1 cup acorn squash, cubed
- 1/2 carrot, thinly sliced
- 1/2 teaspoon smoked paprika

Directions

1. Stir all ingredients, except the corn, into your slow cooker. Cook on Low for 7 hours 30 minutes.
2. Then, throw in the corn. Continue to cook on Low for 40 minutes longer.
3. Serve topped with shredded Cheddar cheese, if desired.

– VEGAN –

113. Summer Bean Salad with Peppers

A vegan diet and slow cooking go hand in hand. This great combo of beans and vegetables proves that. Just follow these simple steps, sit down and enjoy a bowl of the best protein salad ever.

Ready in about
2 hours
40 minutes

NUTRITIONAL INFORMATION
(Per Serving)

389 - Calories
8.1g - Fat
63.9g - Carbs
19.9g - Protein
12.3g - Sugars

Ingredients

For the Salad:
- 1/2 red bell pepper, chopped
- 1/2 red onion, cut into thin rings
- 6 ounces canned dark red kidney beans, drained and rinsed
- 1/2 green bell peppers, chopped
- 1/4 cup water
- 1 cup green beans
- 5 ounces canned chickpeas, drained and rinsed

For the Dressing:
- 1/2 teaspoon fresh basil, minced
- 1/2 tablespoon olive oil
- 1 fresh scallions, chopped
- 1 tablespoon lime juice
- 1 clove garlic, minced
- Sea salt and freshly ground black pepper, to your taste
- 1/2 tablespoon wine vinegar

Directions

1. Place all salad ingredients in your slow cooker. Give it a good stir.
2. Then, slow cook for 2 hours 30 minutes on High setting. Drain the contents of the slow cooker and allow it to cool completely.
3. Meanwhile, in a small-sized bowl, whisk all items for the dressing. Whisk until everything is thoroughly combined. Pour the dressing over the beans. Toss and serve well chilled.

– VEGAN –

114. Tangy Red Cabbage

Enjoy this perfectly cooked red cabbage with the best aromatics. Serve alongside a homemade corn bread and a fresh salad.

Ready in about
5 hours
40 minutes

NUTRITIONAL INFORMATION
(Per Serving)

161 - Calories
10.3g - Fat
15.8g - Carbs
2.7g - Protein
9.2g - Sugars

Ingredients

- 1/2 medium onion, shredded
- 1/4 cup apple cider vinegar
- 1/2 head red cabbage, shredded
- 1 tablespoon vegetable oil
- 1/4 teaspoon cayenne pepper
- 2 tablespoons water
- 1/4 teaspoon freshly ground black pepper
- 1/2 tablespoon dark brown sugar
- 1/2 teaspoon ground bay leaf
- 1/2 teaspoon dried marjoram
- 1/4 teaspoon salt, to taste

Directions

1. Just throw all ingredients into your slow cooker. Give it a good stir.
2. Cook on Low approximately 5 hours 30 minutes.
3. Stir before serving and enjoy!

– VEGAN –

115. Rich and Flavorful Three-Bean Chili with Corn

Three-bean chili is always a good idea for an amazing Sunday lunch. Slow-cooked chili is one of the best ways to comfort yourself and your beloved one.

Ready in about 8 hours

NUTRITIONAL INFORMATION
(Per Serving)

326 - Calories
1.5g - Fat
63.4g - Carbs
19.5g - Protein
10.4g - Sugars

Ingredients

- 10 ounces canned tomatoes, diced
- 1 teaspoon fresh jalapeño, finely minced
- 4 ounces canned black beans, drained and rinsed
- 1/2 large-sized carrot, diced
- 1 clove garlic, minced
- 5 ounces canned cannellini beans, drained and rinsed
- 1/2 stalk celery, diced
- 5 ounces canned kidney beans, drained and rinsed
- 1/2 teaspoon chili powder
- 1/2 teaspoon cumin
- 1 teaspoon jalapeño hot sauce
- 1/2 teaspoon smoked cayenne pepper
- 1/2 parsnip, chopped
- 1/2 teaspoon smoked paprika
- 1/2 cup fresh corn kernels
- 1/2 onion, diced

Directions

1. Place all ingredients, except the corn, in your slow cooker. Slow cook on Low for 7 hours 30 minutes.
2. Stir in the corn. Cover and continue to cook for 20 minutes more on Low setting. Stir before serving and enjoy!

FAST SNACKS & APPETIZERS

116. Easy Boiled Peanuts

Use Virginia or Valencia peanuts in this recipe! You can easily double or triple this recipe as well.

Ready in about
6 hours
30 minutes

NUTRITIONAL INFORMATION
(Per Serving)

621 - Calories
53.9g - Fat
17.7g - Carbs
28.3g - Protein
4.4g - Sugars

Ingredients

- 2 ½ cups water
- 1 ½ cups green peanuts, uncooked
- 2 tablespoons sea salt

Directions

1. Place all of the above ingredients in your slow cooker and stir to combine.
2. Cook, covered, on High for 6 hours. Pour in additional water during cooking, if necessary. Enjoy!

117. Classic Caramel Fondue

Seriously, how can you go wrong with classic caramel fondue? You might need to make a double batch because it disappears almost as fast as you can make it!

Ready in about
2 hours
40 minutes

NUTRITIONAL INFORMATION
(Per Serving)

338 - Calories
10.2g - Fat
58.2g - Carbs
3.3g - Protein
43.9g - Sugars

Ingredients

- 1/4 cup milk
- 8 mini marshmallows
- 1/8 teaspoon cinnamon
- 10 caramel bites
- 1/8 teaspoon salt

Directions

1. Throw all of the ingredients into your slow cooker; cover with the lid.
2. Cook on Low for 2 hours 30 minutes, stirring periodically.
3. Serve with some fruits or cakes on the side.

118. Broccoli and Water Chestnut Dip

Water chestnuts are a good source of fiber, vitamin B6, riboflavin, potassium, copper, and vitamin A. Broccoli is a nutrient-packed food with β-carotene compounds, dietary fiber and valuable vitamins.

Ready in about 40 minutes

NUTRITIONAL INFORMATION
(Per Serving)

219 - Calories
16.7g - Fat
15.7g - Carbs
3.6g - Protein
3.7g - Sugars

Ingredients

- 1/4 stick butter
- 1/2 carrot, chopped
- 1/2 teaspoon Worcestershire sauce
- 1/2 celery rib, chopped
- 1/4 cup cream of celery soup
- 3 ounces frozen broccoli florets
- 1/2 onion, chopped
- 2 tablespoons cream cheese
- 1/4 cup water chestnuts, sliced

Directions

1. Boil broccoli florets until just tender, about 15 minutes. Sauté onion, carrot, and celery until tender. Transfer the sautéed vegetables to the slow cooker.
2. Then, stir in the butter, cream cheese, and celery soup. Then, heat on Low until cheese is melted, about 15 minutes.
3. Now, stir in the water chestnuts and Worcestershire sauce. Serve warm with your favorite dippers.

119. Candied Coconut Banana

Delicious for simple snacks or garnishes, dipped in sauce, candied banana is worth the effort. In this recipe, you can add a dash of brandy as well as 2-3 whole cloves.

Ready in about 40 minutes

NUTRITIONAL INFORMATION
(Per Serving)

230 - Calories
7.9g - Fat
42.6g - Carbs
1.6g - Protein
20g - Sugars

Ingredients

- 2 tablespoons coconut flakes
- 1 tablespoon butter, melted
- 1 tablespoon lemon juice
- 2 bananas, peeled
- 1/8 teaspoon sea salt
- 1/2 teaspoon grated lemon peel
- 1/4 teaspoon cinnamon
- 2 tablespoons corn syrup

Directions

1. Throw the banana and coconut into your slow cooker. Sprinkle cinnamon and sea salt over the top.
2. In a mixing bowl, combine the corn syrup, butter, lemon juice, and lemon peel; pour the mixture over your bananas.
3. Cover and cook on Low setting for 2 hours 30 minutes.

– FAST SNACKS & APPETIZERS –

120. Apple and Mustard Cocktail Kielbasa

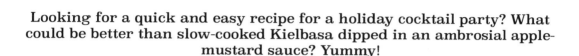

Looking for a quick and easy recipe for a holiday cocktail party? What could be better than slow-cooked Kielbasa dipped in an ambrosial apple-mustard sauce? Yummy!

Ready in about
2 hours
40 minutes

NUTRITIONAL INFORMATION
(Per Serving)

390 - Calories
14g - Fat
55.9g - Carbs
11.1g - Protein
35.3g - Sugars

Ingredients

- 5 ounces apple jelly
- 3 ounces Kielbasa, sliced
- 1 ounce mustard

Directions

1. Throw sliced Kielbasa into your slow cooker.
2. In a mixing dish, combine the apple jelly and mustard. Pour the mixture over Kielbasa in the slow cooker.
3. Set your cooker on Low setting; cook for 2 hours 30 minutes, stirring occasionally. Serve and enjoy!

121. The Best Spiced Cashews Ever

Cashews are an appetite-suppressing food and a great solution for minimizing your hunger between meals. Sure, you can come up with your own spice combinations.

Ready in about
3 hours
10 minutes

NUTRITIONAL INFORMATION
(Per Serving)

447 - Calories
37.5g - Fat
23.1g - Carbs
10.6g - Protein
4.2g - Sugars

Ingredients

- 1 tablespoon butter, melted
- 1/2 teaspoon brown sugar
- 1/4 teaspoon cayenne pepper
- 1/4 teaspoon salt
- 1/4 teaspoon garlic powder
- 1 cup cashews
- 1 tablespoon dried rosemary, crushed
- 1/4 teaspoon cumin
- 1/8 teaspoon ground black pepper
- 1/4 teaspoon shallot powder

Directions

1. Heat your slow cooker for 13 minutes on High; then, place cashews in the slow cooker. Now, combine brown sugar, salt and all seasonings; toss to coat.
2. Drizzle melted butter over all. Cover and slow cook on Low setting about 2 hours 30 minutes, stirring every 30 minutes.
3. Next, open the lid and cook for 20 minutes longer, stirring periodically.
4. Transfer to a nice serving bowl, serve at room temperature and enjoy!

– FAST SNACKS & APPETIZERS –

122. Curry Pepper Almonds

Almonds are packed with dietary fiber, antioxidants, riboflavin, and magnesium. These amazing nuts can help prevent heart diseases and diabetes; they can boost brain function and prevent obesity.

Ready in about 3 hours

NUTRITIONAL INFORMATION
(Per Serving)

300 - Calories
26.6g - Fat
10.2g - Carbs
10.1g - Protein
2g - Sugars

Ingredients

- 1/4 teaspoon garlic powder
- 1/2 tablespoon butter, melted
- 1 cup whole almonds
- Sea salt, to your liking
- 1/2 teaspoon curry powder
- 1/4 teaspoon ground red peppercorns
- 1/4 teaspoon ground black peppercorns
- 1/4 teaspoon ground green peppercorns

Directions

1. Heat your slow cooker for 13 minutes on High; add your almonds. Drizzle melted butter over the almonds; toss to coat.
2. Sprinkle curry powder, garlic powder, and ground peppercorns over them; add sea salt and toss again until everything is well coated. Turn the heat to Low setting; cook, covered, 1 hour 30 minutes; make sure to stir every 30 minutes.
3. Increase heat to High; uncover and cook 1 hour longer, stirring every 15 minutes.
4. Serve at room temperature or store in a sealed container for up to 3 weeks. Enjoy!

– FAST SNACKS & APPETIZERS –

123. Curried Cheese and Cranberry Dip

This dipping sauce is extra-creamy and so easy to prepare. You just need to throw all ingredients into your cooker. Monterey Jack cheese works well too.

Ready in about 2 hours 45 minutes

NUTRITIONAL INFORMATION (Per Serving)

358 - Calories
21.2g - Fat
17.2g - Carbs
25.3g - Protein
7.2g - Sugars

Ingredients

- 2 tablespoons mango chutney, chopped
- 3/4 cup Swiss cheese, shredded
- 1 clove garlic, minced
- 1 green onion, finely chopped
- 1 cup Ricotta cheese
- 1/2 teaspoon curry powder
- 1 tablespoon dried cranberries

Directions

1. Place Ricotta cheese and Swiss cheese in your slow cooker; cover and cook about 35 minutes or until the cheeses are fully melted.
2. Then, add the remaining ingredients. Cover with the lid and cook 2 hours longer.
3. Serve with veggie sticks of choice.

– FAST SNACKS & APPETIZERS –

124. Candied Mixed Nuts

If you're looking for a variety of nuts in one bowl, give this recipe a try. Slow cooking is much easier and better way to make these nuts than the stovetop method. Your nuts are perfectly cooked with no bitter burned spots.

Ready in about
2 hours
40 minutes

NUTRITIONAL INFORMATION
(Per Serving)

524 - Calories
37.3g - Fat
40.9g - Carbs
14.9g - Protein
27.5g - Sugars

Ingredients

- 1/2 egg white
- 2 tablespoons almonds
- 1/4 teaspoon freshly grated nutmeg
- 1/2 cup cashews
- 1/4 teaspoon pure vanilla extract
- 1/4 teaspoon ground cinnamon
- 1/4 teaspoon pure coconut extract
- 1/2 cup walnuts
- 2 tablespoons water
- 1/4 cup sugar

Directions

1. Place the walnuts, cashews, and almond in your slow cooker that is greased with a nonstick spray.
2. In a mixing bowl, combine together the sugar, nutmeg, and cinnamon. Sprinkle the mixture over the nuts in the slow cooker.
3. In another mixing bowl, beat the egg white with vanilla extract and coconut extract.
4. Cook, covered, 2 hours 30 minutes on Low setting, stirring every 20 minutes. Lastly, pour water into the slow cooker during last 20 minutes.
5. Allow candied nuts to cool slightly before serving. Enjoy!

– FAST SNACKS & APPETIZERS –

125. Cheesy Artichoke and Spinach Dipping Sauce

(If you love artichokes and cheese in the same dish, give this recipe a try. This out-of-the-box combination will blow your mind!

Ready in about
1 hour
50 minutes

NUTRITIONAL INFORMATION
(Per Serving)

195 - Calories
13.1g - Fat
9.6g - Carbs
8.7g - Protein
3.3g - Sugars

Ingredients

- 1/4 cup canned artichoke hearts, drained and chopped
- 1 clove garlic, crushed
- 2 tablespoons Chèvre cheese, room temperature
- 1/2 small-sized onion, sliced
- 1/8 teaspoon freshly cracked black pepper
- 1/2 teaspoon dried dill weed
- 1/4 teaspoon sea salt
- 1/4 teaspoon dried thyme
- 1/4 teaspoon dried rosemary, crushed
- 1/2 teaspoon balsamic vinegar
- 1/4 cup Pecorino Romano, grated
- 1/4 teaspoon cayenne pepper
- 1 cup spinach leaves, torn into pieces
- 2 tablespoons mayonnaise

Directions

1. Melt Pecorino Romano and Chèvre cheese in your slow cooker on Low setting; it will take about 35 minutes until the cheeses are fully melted.
2. Then, add the rest of the above ingredients; cook for 1 hour 10 minutes longer.
3. Serve with your favorite dippers.

BEANS & GRAINS

– Beans & Grains –

126. Light and Aromatic Breakfast Risotto

Jasmine rice works greatest for this recipe but you can freely use any type of white rice. You can also add 1-2 tablespoons of minced spring garlic if desired.

Ready in about
1 hour
40 minutes

NUTRITIONAL INFORMATION
(Per Serving)

296 - Calories
12.6g - Fat
22.5g - Carbs
13.4g - Protein
1.2g - Sugars

Ingredients

- 1 cup vegetable broth
- Salt and freshly ground black pepper, to your liking
- 1/4 cup Parmesan cheese, freshly grated
- 1 green onion, finely chopped
- 1/4 teaspoon garlic powder
- 1/4 cup water
- 1/2 teaspoon dried basil
- 1 tablespoon butter or margarine
- 1 teaspoon paprika
- 1/2 cup dry white wine
- 1 cup jasmine rice

Directions

1. In a saucepan, melt 1/2 tablespoon of the butter (margarine) over medium-high heat; then, sauté green onion until it's softened. Stir in the rice and raise the heat to high.
2. Next, pour in the wine, and cook, stirring periodically, for about 6 minutes.
3. Transfer the rice mixture to the slow cooker. Pour in the water and broth. Cover the slow cooker and cook on High for 1 hour 30 minutes.
4. Now, uncover and add the remaining ingredients, including the remaining butter (margarine). Give it a good stir.
5. Taste, adjust the seasonings, and serve right away.

– BEANS & GRAINS –

127. Classic Grits with Swiss Cheese

As a matter of fact, grits are a stone-ground cornmeal dish that can be served in so many ways. These grits with cheese are delicious enough to have as breakfast and healthy enough to serve for dinner without any guilt.

Ready in about 7 hours 40 minutes

NUTRITIONAL INFORMATION
(Per Serving)

108 - Calories
7.1g - Fat
6.6g - Carbs
4.4g - Protein
0.9g - Sugars

Ingredients

- 2 cups water
- Salt and freshly ground black pepper, to your liking
- 1/2 tablespoon butter
- 1/2 cup stone-ground grits
- 2 tablespoons Swiss cheese, shredded

Directions

1. Add the grits, water, butter, salt, and black pepper to your slow cooker. Stir until everything is well incorporated.
2. Cook for 7 hours 30 minutes on Low setting. Top with Swiss cheese and serve warm.

128. Autumn Harvest Oatmeal

In this recipe, we opted for apples and pears; you can use berries, fresh or dried, as well. Did you know that October 29th is National Oatmeal Day?

Ready in about
8 hours
10 minutes

NUTRITIONAL INFORMATION
(Per Serving)

165 - Calories
1.7g - Fat
35.9g - Carbs
2.9g - Protein
16.8g - Sugars

Ingredients

- 1 cup old-fashioned rolled oats
- 1/2 tablespoon sugar
- 1 pear, cored and sliced thinly
- 1/8 teaspoon cinnamon
- 1/2 apple, cored and sliced thinly
- 1/4 teaspoon ground cloves
- 1 cup water
- 1/4 teaspoon vanilla paste
- 2 tablespoons pear cider

Directions

1. Put all ingredients into your slow cooker. Cook on Low overnight or for 8 hours.
2. Serve warm and enjoy.

– BEANS & GRAINS –

129. Habanero Turkey Chili

This is not ordinary chili. The addition of ground turkey and habanero hot sauce in this recipe turns an everyday taste into something memorable!

Ready in about
9 hours
20 minutes

NUTRITIONAL INFORMATION
(Per Serving)

452 - Calories
4.7g - Fat
61.4g - Carbs
42.4g - Protein
4.6g - Sugars

Ingredients

- 6 ounces canned diced tomatoes
- 1/2 teaspoon soy sauce
- 2 green onions, chopped
- Salt and ground black pepper, to your taste
- 8 ounces canned red kidney beans, drained and rinsed
- 1 cup turkey, ground
- 1/2 teaspoon smoked cayenne pepper
- 1/2 teaspoon cumin
- 1 clove garlic, chopped
- 1/2 tablespoon habanero hot sauce
- 1 chipotle chilies in adobo

Directions

1. In a nonstick skillet, quickly sauté the turkey until thoroughly warmed. Drain all excess fat and transfer the meat to the slow cooker.
2. Add all ingredients to the slow cooker. Stir until everything's well combined. Cook for 9 hours on Low setting.

130. Overnight Oatmeal with Dried Cherries

This tasty overnight oatmeal can be thrown together in a snap, using convenient and inexpensive basics! Include this recipe in your weekly meal plan and you will experience numerous health benefits! Serve with honey or agave syrup if desired.

Ready in about 9 hours 20 minutes

NUTRITIONAL INFORMATION (Per Serving)

161 - Calories
3g - Fat
29.6g - Carbs
5g - Protein
1g - Sugars

Ingredients

- 1 cup old-fashioned rolled oats
- 1/4 teaspoon cinnamon powder
- 1/4 cup dried cherries
- 1/8 teaspoon ground cloves
- 3 cups water

Directions

1. Throw all of the above ingredients into your slow cooker. Then, set the slow cooker to Low heat.
2. Now, slow cook overnight or 9 hours and serve warm. Enjoy!

– BEANS & GRAINS –

131. Slow Cooker Muesli Mix

This recipe calls for different cereals in order to achieve a rich and layered flavor. Top each serving with a scoop of Greek-style yogurt and enjoy!

Ready in about 2 hours

NUTRITIONAL INFORMATION
(Per Serving)

411 - Calories
15.6g - Fat
57.8g - Carbs
11.7g - Protein
19.2g - Sugars

Ingredients

- 1 tablespoon canola oil
- 1/2 teaspoon pure vanilla extract
- 2 tablespoons dried cranberries
- 2 tablespoons wheat germ
- 1/4 cup coconut meat, shredded
- 2 tablespoons honey
- 1/2 cup baking natural bran
- 1/2 tablespoon flax seeds
- 1 cup rolled oats

Directions

1. Preheat your slow cooker on High for 15 minutes.
2. Add all of the ingredients to the slow cooker and stir thoroughly.
3. Now cook, covered, on High for about 1 hour 30 minutes, stirring once or twice. Serve warm.

132. Nutty Overnight Porridge

Here is a simple porridge recipe that is actually lip-smacking good! This old-fashioned porridge evokes childhood memories.

Ready in about
9 hours
10 minutes

NUTRITIONAL INFORMATION
(Per Serving)

254 - Calories
8.4g - Fat
38.7g - Carbs
7.6g - Protein
17.3g - Sugars

Ingredients

- 2 cups water
- 2 tablespoons walnuts, toasted and coarsely chopped
- 1/8 teaspoon ground allspice
- 1/4 teaspoon pure vanilla extract
- 1 cinnamon sticks
- 3/4 cup rolled oats
- 2 tablespoons brown sugar, or to taste
- 1/2 cup full cream milk
- 1/8 teaspoon kosher salt

Directions

1. In your slow cooker, combine the oats, water, cinnamon sticks, and kosher salt. Set the slow cooker on Low, cover, and let cook overnight, or 9 hours.
2. In the morning, stir in the remaining items. Scoop the porridge into serving bowls. Serve and enjoy!

– BEANS & GRAINS –

133. Muesli with Black Currants and Seeds

Inspired by coconut and dried fruits, you can come up with this breakfast idea that's so easy and literally scrumptious! This recipe calls for fresh coconut; you can substitute it for coconut flakes.

Ready in about
1 hour
50 minutes

NUTRITIONAL INFORMATION
(Per Serving)

472 - Calories
17.5g - Fat
64.3g - Carbs
17.2g - Protein
23.5g - Sugars

Ingredients

- 1 tablespoon butter, room temperature
- 1 tablespoon sesame seeds
- 2 tablespoons dried black currants
- 1/2 cup rolled oats
- 2 tablespoons maple syrup
- 1/2 cup baking natural bran
- 1/2 teaspoon pure vanilla extract
- 1/2 tablespoon sunflower seeds
- 1/2 cup wheat germ
- 1/4 cup coconut
- 1/4 teaspoon pure coconut extract

Directions

1. Set your slow cooker to High heat for 15 minutes.
2. Add all of the above items to the lightly greased and preheated slow cooker.
3. Then, cook, covered, on High for 1 hours 30 minutes, stirring occasionally. Serve and enjoy.

— Beans & Grains —

134. Grandma's Butter Cornbread

Corn meal is loaded with fiber, phosphorus, iron, and other essential nutrients. Here's just one of many amazing recipes that include this superfood.

Ready in about
2 hours
40 minutes

NUTRITIONAL INFORMATION
(Per Serving)

472 - Calories
10.5g - Fat
80.5g - Carbs
14.8g - Protein
7.9g - Sugars

Ingredients

- 1 egg
- 1/8 teaspoon allspice
- 1/2 cup cornmeal
- 1/4 teaspoon baking soda
- 1/4 teaspoon salt
- 1 tablespoon butter
- 3/4 cup buttermilk
- 1/2 tablespoon sugar
- 1/2 tablespoon baking powder
- 1 cup all-purpose flour

Directions

1. Warm the butter in your slow cooker over medium-high heat.
2. In a medium-sized mixing dish, combine together the flour, cornmeal, baking soda, baking powder, and sugar.
3. Now, stir in the salt, allspice, buttermilk, and egg. Stir to combine well.
4. Pour the batter into the slow cooker and spread evenly. Cover and cook for 2 hours 30 minutes on High heat setting.
5. Allow your cornbread to cool slightly before slicing and serving. Enjoy!

– BEANS & GRAINS –

135. Dinner Turkey Chili

When you're looking for just the right thing to serve in the late afternoon in autumn, give this recipe a try. You can use the ground pepper instead of peppercorns, and add 1-2 garlic cloves if desired.

Ready in about
8 hours
40 minutes

NUTRITIONAL INFORMATION
(Per Serving)

241 - Calories
2.8g - Fat
21.8g - Carbs
31.5g - Protein
6.3g - Sugars

Ingredients

- 1/2 small-sized turkey breast, cooked and cubed
- 1/2 teaspoon cumin
- 3 green peppercorns
- 1/2 teaspoon paprika
- 1/2 teaspoon kosher salt
- 1/2 teaspoon fennel seeds
- 1/4 teaspoon freshly ground black pepper
- 1/4 cup scallions, chopped
- 1/4 cup canned cannellini beans, drained and rinsed
- 1/2 teaspoon apple cider vinegar
- 1 ounce drained canned green peppers

Directions

1. Place all items, except the turkey, in your slow cooker. Stir to mix well.
2. Cook on Low for 7 hours 30 minutes.
3. Once the time is up, add the turkey breast. Continue to cook on High for an additional 1 hour. Serve right away.

DESSERTS

– DESSERTS –

136. Every Day Cashew Banana Foster

Banana Foster was originally invented in 1951 by Paul Blangé at Brennan's in New Orleans. Since then, this amazing dessert has been served worldwide. Serve warm over your favorite ice cream.

Ready in about 2 hours 20 minutes

NUTRITIONAL INFORMATION
(Per Serving)

418 - Calories
19.9g - Fat
54.7g - Carbs
4.1g - Protein
37.2g - Sugars

Ingredients

- 1/4 cup brown sugar
- 1/2 teaspoon vanilla extract
- 1/4 cup cashews, chopped
- 1/2 tablespoon raw honey
- 1/4 teaspoon pure hazelnut extract
- 1/4 teaspoon ground cinnamon
- 2 large-sized bananas, sliced
- 2 tablespoons butter, melted
- 2 tablespoons brandy

Directions

1. Arrange sliced bananas on the bottom of a lightly buttered slow cooker.
2. In a mixing bowl, combine the butter, brown sugar, honey, and brandy; mix until it's thoroughly combined.
3. Next, whisk in the hazelnut extract, vanilla and cinnamon; pour the hazelnut mixture over bananas in the slow cooker.
4. Cover and slow cook for 1 hour 30 minutes on Low setting. Top with cashews and cook for 40 minutes more. Bon appétit!

– DESSERTS –

137. Light and Easy Pumpkin Pie

No more excuses for not making desserts! Even a pumpkin pie with a special holiday flavor! Enjoy!

Ready in about
3 hours
40 minutes

NUTRITIONAL INFORMATION
(Per Serving)

314 - Calories
12.6g - Fat
43.5g - Carbs
9.1g - Protein
28.2g - Sugars

Ingredients

- 1 tablespoon melted butter
- 4 ounces evaporated milk
- 1/4 cup all-purpose flour
- 1/4 teaspoon baking powder
- 5 ounces pumpkin
- A pinch of salt
- 1 egg, beaten
- 1/2 teaspoon ground cinnamon
- 1/4 teaspoon freshly grated nutmeg
- 1/4 cup coconut sugar

Directions

1. Combine all ingredients in your slow cooker.
2. Then, seal the slow cooker and cook the mixture for 3 hours 30 minutes on Low setting. Serve chilled and enjoy!

– DESSERTS –

138. Aunt's Two-Chocolate Fudge

When you are in a hurry or you're just not in the mood to cook, it's good to have this recipe on hand. Everyone can throw the ingredients into the slow cooker and set the timer, right?!

Ready in about 55 minutes + chilling time

NUTRITIONAL INFORMATION
(Per Serving)

424 - Calories
19g - Fat
61.6g - Carbs
4.1g - Protein
29.9g - Sugars

Ingredients

- 2 tablespoons honey
- 1/8 teaspoon mace
- 1/4 cup white chocolate chips
- 1/4 teaspoon pure vanilla extract
- 3/4 cup milk chocolate chips
- 2 tablespoons heavy whipping cream
- 1/8 teaspoon salt
- 1/4 teaspoon pure almond extract

Directions

1. Stir milk chocolate chips, heavy whipping cream, and honey into the slow cooker. Cover and cook for 50 minutes on High heat.
2. Stir in white chocolate chips; stir until the chocolate melts. Add the remaining ingredients.
3. Pour the mixture into a foil-lined baking dish. Allow it to cool at least 4 hours. Cut into squares and serve.

– DESSERTS –

139. Brownie Pudding Cake

Inspired by black chocolate, you can come up with this dessert idea that's so easy and literally scrumptious! This recipe calls for fresh grated ginger; you can substitute it for a crystalized ginger.

Ready in about
2 hours
40 minutes

NUTRITIONAL
INFORMATION
(Per Serving)

497 - Calories
24.4g - Fat
61.9g - Carbs
11.2g - Protein
33.1g - Sugars

Ingredients

- 2 tablespoons canola oil
- 2 tablespoons toasted almonds, coarsely chopped
- 1/4 teaspoon salt
- 2 tablespoons baking cocoa
- 1 whole egg
- 1 egg white
- 1/4 cup granulated sugar
- 1 ounce bittersweet chocolate, room temperature
- 1/2 cup flour
- 1/2 teaspoon baking soda
- Powdered sugar, if desired
- 1/2 teaspoon vanilla essence

Directions

1. In bowl, combine the flour, sugar, salt, baking soda, and cocoa. In another mixing bowl, stir the oil, vanilla essence, egg, and egg whites; beat with a wire whisk.
2. Add the egg/vanilla mixture to the flour mixture; stir until everything is well blended. Stir in the chocolate and almonds.
3. Grease your slow cooker with a nonstick spray. Scrape the batter into the slow cooker.
4. Seal the slow cooker; cook on Low setting for 2 hours 10 minutes. Turn off the cooker. Allow it to stand covered for 20 minutes before serving.
5. Dust with powdered sugar before serving.

– DESSERTS –

140. Chocolate Nut Clusters

Add a festive look to your dessert table every day with these appetizing clusters. Almond bark is actually a chocolate-like ingredient made with vegetable fats instead of cocoa butter.

Ready in about 5 hours

NUTRITIONAL INFORMATION
(Per Serving)

565 - Calories
40.2g - Fat
40.6g - Carbs
13.3g - Protein
32.3g - Sugars

Ingredients

- 4 ounces chocolate-flavored candy coating (almond bark)
- 2 ounces almonds
- 2 ounces peanuts
- 2 ounces package vanilla-flavored candy coating

Directions

1. In a slow cooker, place candy coatings. Seal the lid; heat on Low setting for 3 hours 20 minutes. Make sure to stir occasionally until everything is well coated.
2. Add the peanuts and almonds, and stir until they are well coated. Drop by tablespoonful onto a cooking parchment. Allow the clusters to set about 1 hour 30 minutes.

– DESSERTS –

141. Apple and Apricot Crumble

It's apple season! For this recipe, use baking apples that offer a balance of sweet and tart flavors such as Granny Smith, Pink Lady, Jonathans or Honey Crisp. If you're out of ideas for an easy and satisfying dessert, give this recipe a try!

Ready in about
1 hour
20 minutes

NUTRITIONAL INFORMATION
(Per Serving)

214 - Calories
5.7g - Fat
40.3g - Carbs
4.2g - Protein
27.2g - Sugars

Ingredients

For the Filling:
- 2 tablespoons walnuts, minced
- 1/8 teaspoon ground cloves
- 1 apple, chopped
- 1/2 teaspoon ground cinnamon
- 2 apricots, pitted and chopped
- 1 tablespoon coconut sugar

For the Topping:
- 1 tablespoon pastry flour
- 1/8 teaspoon ginger, ground
- 1/2 tablespoon milk
- 3 tablespoons rolled oats
- 1/2 teaspoon vanilla essence
- 1 tablespoon granulated sugar

Directions

1. Combine all the filling components in a lightly oiled slow cooker.
2. In a mixing dish, combine all the topping components; stir thoroughly until everything's well combined.
3. Now, drop the topping mixture by teaspoons on top of the filling in the slow cooker.
4. Cook for 1 hour 10 minutes on High setting. Serve with double cream. Enjoy!

– DESSERTS –

142. Peach and Sweet Potato Pudding

There are so many ways to serve this delectable pudding. Spoon it on top of your favorite ice cream or serve with pancakes. The possibilities are endless!

Ready in about
7 hours
40 minutes

NUTRITIONAL INFORMATION
(Per Serving)

479 - Calories
12.9g - Fat
84.5g - Carbs
9.8g - Protein
43g - Sugars

Ingredients

- 1 tablespoon butter
- 1/4 teaspoon mace
- 4 ounces canned evaporated milk
- 4 ounces canned peaches with juice, crushed
- 1/4 teaspoon orange extract
- 1/2 pound sweet potatoes shredded
- 1/2 teaspoon ground cloves
- 1 egg, beaten
- 1/4 teaspoon vanilla paste
- 1/4 cup sugar
- 1/2 tablespoon honey
- 1/2 teaspoon pumpkin pie spice mix

Directions

1. Lightly oil your slow cooker with a nonstick cooking spray. Then, combine peaches, sweet potatoes, evaporated milk, sugar, and honey in a bowl; whisk to combine well.
2. Then, throw in the egg and butter. Add the remaining ingredients. Whisk to combine well.
3. Seal the cooker and cook on Low for 7 hours 30 minutes; make sure to stir every 2 hours. Serve and enjoy.

– DESSERTS –

143. Coconut Hot Chocolate

Hot chocolate is very customizable and easy to make confection! You can enjoy this silky and sophisticated hot chocolate all year long.

Ready in about 2 hours 30 minutes

NUTRITIONAL INFORMATION
(Per Serving)

468 - Calories
22.4g - Fat
70.8g - Carbs
1.9g - Protein
64.2g - Sugars

Ingredients

- 3/4 can full-fat coconut milk
- 1 cup coconut milk
- 1/4 ounce cinnamon
- 1/4 teaspoon mace
- 1/2 cup coconut sugar
- 1/3 cup coconut cream
- 2 ounces semisweet chocolate, chopped

Directions

1. Simply throw all ingredients into your slow cooker. Turn the cooker on High setting.
2. Then, cook about 2 hours 20 minutes.
3. Divide your hot chocolate among 2 mugs and serve immediately. Enjoy!

– DESSERTS –

144. Winter Hazelnut Fudge Sauce

A fudge sauce is an impressive dessert that is extra easy to make in your slow cooker. Once you taste how good this dessert is, it will become a staple for your holiday menu. Garnish with chopped hazelnuts.

Ready in about
2 hours
20 minutes

NUTRITIONAL INFORMATION
(Per Serving)

388 - Calories
22.1g - Fat
39.4g - Carbs
8.2g - Protein
34.9g - Sugars

Ingredients

- 4 ounces bittersweet chocolate chips
- 1/4 teaspoon grated nutmeg
- 1/8 teaspoon salt
- 1/2 teaspoon butter
- 1/2 teaspoon cinnamon
- 1/2 teaspoon vanilla paste
- 1/4 teaspoon pure hazelnut extract
- 4 ounces evaporated milk

Directions

1. Throw all ingredients into the slow cooker. Cook on Low, stirring every 15 minutes, for 2 hours 15 minutes.
2. Serve over ice cream. Keep the fudge sauce in a jar in the refrigerator, because it reheats well.

– DESSERTS –

145. Easy Berry Cobbler

Make a berry cobbler a little more excessive by adding a scoop of fine ice cream on the side. In this recipe, you can use dried cherries instead of cranberries and get the great result too.

Ready in about
3 hours
40 minutes

NUTRITIONAL INFORMATION
(Per Serving)

370 - Calories
26.5g - Fat
32.6g - Carbs
2g - Protein
19g Sugars

Ingredients

- 1/2 stick butter, melted
- 1/4 cup dried cranberries
- 1/2 box yellow cake mix
- 1/2 cup raspberries
- 1/4 teaspoon ground cloves
- 1/4 cup strawberries, quartered
- 1 tablespoon coconut sugar

Directions

1. Treat your slow cooker with a nonstick cooking spray. In a large-sized mixing bowl, combine all of the above ingredients.
2. Press the mixture into the slow cooker. Cover and cook approximately 3 hours 30 minutes on Low heat setting.

– DESSERTS –

146. Coconut Rice Pudding with Prunes

This totally decadent pudding is a must-have for Sunday afternoon! You can soak prunes in 1-2 tablespoons of brandy for about 30 minutes before using them.

Ready in about 2 hours 40 minutes

NUTRITIONAL INFORMATION
(Per Serving)

332 - Calories
15.3g - Fat
49.3g - Carbs
3.5g - Protein
25.8g - Sugars

Ingredients

- 3 tablespoons jasmine rice
- 2 tablespoons coconut water
- 1 tablespoon coconut sugar
- 1 carrot, grated
- 1 tablespoon shredded coconut
- 1/4 teaspoon mace
- 1/4 teaspoon cinnamon
- 1/2 cup coconut milk
- 1/2 teaspoon almond extract
- 1/8 teaspoon kosher salt
- 3 prunes, pitted and chopped

Directions

1. Dump all of the above ingredients into the slow cooker.
2. Cook for 2 hours 30 minutes on High, till the rice becomes tender.
3. Stir before serving and serve in individual bowls. Enjoy!

– DESSERTS –

147. Vanilla Orange Custard

Easy and delicious custard at your fingertips! A slow cooker turns regular custard into a royally luxurious dessert. Add a sprinkle of freshly grated nutmeg just before serving.

Ready in about
7 hours
40 minutes

NUTRITIONAL
INFORMATION
(Per Serving)

238 - Calories
11.5g - Fat
22g - Carbs
12g - Protein
22g - Sugars

Ingredients

- 1/4 teaspoon pure orange extract
- 2 eggs
- 2 tablespoons sugar
- 1/2 teaspoon pure vanilla extract
- 3/4 cup fat-free evaporated milk

Directions

1. Place all ingredients in a mixing dish. Whisk until everything is thoroughly combined.
2. Pour the mixture into the slow cooker. Cook on Low for 7 hours 30 minutes, or until it is set. Enjoy!

– DESSERTS –

148. Delectable Crème Brûlée

If you have just found out that you can make the best Crème Brûlée in your slow cooker, you probably feel great! You need just a few simple ingredients to make this French classic.

Ready in about
3 hours
40 minutes

NUTRITIONAL INFORMATION
(Per Serving)

327 - Calories
14.6g - Fat
40.6g - Carbs
12g - Protein
37.9g - Sugars

Ingredients

- 2 egg yolks
- 1/4 cup plus 1 tablespoon sugar
- 1/4 teaspoon vanilla extract
- 1 cup evaporated milk
- 1/2 teaspoon almond extract
- 1 ½ tablespoons cocoa
- 1/2 teaspoon ground cinnamon

Directions

1. In a bowl, whisk the milk, cocoa, almond extract, vanilla, cinnamon, egg yolks, and 1/4 cup of sugar until the sugar dissolves.
2. Pour the mixture into a pan and cook, bringing it to a boil.
3. After that, allow the mixture to cool. Divide the mixture among four broiler-safe ramekins.
4. Pour the water into the bottom of the slow cooker. Lay the ramekins in the water. Cook on High for 3 hours 30 minutes.
5. Lastly, divide the remaining 1 tablespoon of sugar among serving portions. Place them under the broiler; broil until the sugar caramelizes.

– DESSERTS –

149. Mom's Secret Chocolate Cake

This is the recipe from the chocolate heaven! In this gorgeous recipe, a good replacement for pecans would be toasted almonds.

Ready in about
1 hour
30 minutes

NUTRITIONAL
INFORMATION
(Per Serving)

336 - Calories
24.3g - Fat
26g - Carbs
5.6g - Protein
14.3g - Sugars

Ingredients

- 1/2 teaspoon butter, malted
- 1/8 teaspoon cardamom
- 2 tablespoons milk
- 1/4 teaspoon orange extract
- 3 tablespoons pecans, chopped
- 1/4 teaspoon baking soda
- 1/4 teaspoon salt
- 1/2 teaspoon vanilla extract
- 3 tablespoons chocolate chips
- 1/4 cup baking mix
- 1/2 teaspoon ground flaxseeds mixed with 1 teaspoon warm water
- 1/2 tablespoon sugar

Directions

1. Line your slow cooker with a parchment paper.
2. In a mixing bowl, combine together the sugar, baking mix, baking soda, salt, and cardamom.
3. In a separate mixing bowl, combine the milk, flaxseed mix, melted butter, orange extract, and vanilla extract. Now, combine dry sugar mixture with wet milk mixture. Stir until everything is thoroughly combined.
4. Stir in the chocolate chips and pecans. Whisk until you get a smooth batter.
5. Scrape the batter into the slow cooker. Now, put a paper towel between the lid and the slow cooker.
6. Cook on High setting for 1 hour 20 minutes. Serve and enjoy.

– DESSERTS –

150. Autumn Pear-Apple Cobbler with Prunes

An old-fashioned cobbler makes a wonderful ending to any meal. Bosc pears are crisp and juicy but Asian pears would work too. Garnish with whipped cream and enjoy!

Ready in about
2 hours
40 minutes

Ingredients

- 2 tablespoons cold butter
- 1/4 cup sugar
- 1/3 box yellow cake mix, dry
- 1 cup Bosc pears, peeled, cored and sliced
- 1/4 cup prunes, pitted and roughly chopped
- 1/4 teaspoon vanilla extract
- 1 cup tart apples like Granny Smith, peeled, cored and sliced
- Nonstick cooking spray
- 1/4 teaspoon mace

Directions

1. Firstly, treat your slow cooker with a cooking spray. Add the slices of pears and apples, sugar and mace; toss to coat.
2. In large-sized bowl, combine dry cake mix with prunes and vanilla extract. Cut in butter using two knives. Spread the mixture on top of the pear/apple mixture.
3. Seal the slow cooker; cook on High heat setting for 2 hours 30 minutes or until the cobbler topping is golden brown. Serve with whipped cream.

Printed in Great Britain
by Amazon